The Sound of
Fashion Thinking

The Sound of Fashion Thinking

Jonathan Faiers

Sternberg Press

To my darlings, Dell and Inez ...
Cheers big ears!

Fashion Thinking

This book explores Fashion Thinking as a new field
of critical inquiry. Fashion Thinking as a methodology
utilizes many of the ways fashion itself is produced.
Exploring a range of contemporary cultural, political,
economic, and social concerns, Fashion Thinking seeks
to acknowledge, utilize, and celebrate the actual practices,
behaviors, and desires essential to, and characteristic of,
the production of fashion. It asks whether these methods
can generate not just clothing but, in recognizing the
power of fashion's multiple operations and procedures,
encourage us to think differently about subjects other
than garments and textiles. It is a method that retains
and utilizes many of the behaviors attendant on
fashion creation in order to free itself from the academic
conventions and limitations fashion theory imposes.
The practical and, indeed, conceptual features of
Fashion Thinking adopt methods inculcated as intrinsic
to the haptic and sensorial processes that form a conduit
between conception and production at all stages of the
design process and manufacturing.

Fashion Thinking is an attempt to acknowledge and
utilize the essentially creative, serendipitous, social,
ludic, and, indeed, pragmatic systems and behaviors
allied to the creation of fashion. It is a way of thinking
that imitates the actual construction of an article
of clothing itself, from initial conception, drafting a
pattern, sourcing the material, and cutting and assembling
that material to produce a garment. In the same way as
cloth can be fashioned into a coat—literally a something
produced from almost nothing—that same material
can easily be unpicked and refashioned or rethought

into a completely new garment or object. This fluidity characterizes Fashion Thinking, approaching each new topic according to specific demands and desires, cutting its cloth accordingly. Fashion Thinking, like fashion itself, is anticipatory, transformative, reciprocal; it aims beyond interdisciplinarity to a state of indisciplinarity. Such a term implies the ability to be among disciplines but also to be outside of, oblivious to, or even unwilling to be "disciplined," preferring to explore the often turbulent, unruly, and, like fashion, invariably seductive margins of disciplines and where they overlap. Fashion Thinking relishes fashion's fluid, osmotic, replicating, and transformative systems, celebrating its glorious connectedness to culture, ritual, skill, performance, emotion, and transformation, fashioning this into a system of thought.

The concept of indisciplinarity mentioned above is indebted to art historian W. J. T. Mitchell's formulation of it some thirty years ago in the essay "Interdisciplinarity and Visual Culture," in which he discusses the potential of the then still-developing field of visual culture. Mistrustful of the wholesale academic adoption of interdisciplinarity, which he suggests can be "a way of seeming to be just a little bit adventurous and even transgressive, but not too much," also besets, I feel, the field of fashion theory, which attempts to insert fashion into a number of disciplinary arenas but ultimately serves to reinforce its separateness from those same arenas, despite its scrutiny through a variety of disciplinary lenses. Most interestingly, Mitchell calls for an understanding and exploration of visual culture as inclusive of the nonvisual, asking "what in culture lies outside vision," perhaps allowing us access to "anti- or extravisible" worlds, which brings us to the "turbulence or incoherence at the inner and outer boundaries of disciplines." Fashion culture, as one of the richest and most fertile constituents of visual culture, and as both subject and operation, is similarly positioned to consider what lies beyond its immediate subject—clothing—to explore fashion's resonance at the borders of disciplines: a resonance that does not rely on an endless succession of spectacles, of one "look" after another, but instead evokes its multisensory origins, where the look of fashion imbricates with the touch of fashion and the sound of fashion.

Considering the etymological development of the term "fashion" itself can prove enlightening, with its dictionary definitions being remarkably extensive and surprising. While some of the term's former meanings and usage may now appear arcane, fashion's range is undeniable. And so, as a subject, fashion can be understood as "make," "build," "shape," "cut," "kind," "sort," "manner," "mode," "way," "mode of action," "behavior," "demeanor," "actions," "gestures," "way," "outward action," "pretense," "current usage," "manners," "customs," "ways," "mode of life, etc., especially as observed in the upper circles of society," "conformity to this," and "fashionable people." As a verb, fashion can be understood as meaning "to give fashion or shape to," "to form," "mold," "shape," "to frame," "to contrive," "manage," "to change the fashion of," "to transform," "to counterfeit," "to subvert," "to accommodate," "to adapt to."

Together with the linguistic extension of terms such as a "fashioner," denoting "one that fashions; especially a tailor, costumier, modiste," a "fashionist," meaning "a follower of the fashions, one who sets the fashions," and a "fashionmonger," as one who "studies and follows the fashions," it quickly becomes apparent that historically "fashion" has demonstrated a suppleness and potential mobility that current perceptions of it as referring primarily to clothing denies. These definitions also immediately make apparent both the emphasis on the haptic implicit within the various definitions of fashion concerned with the physical act of making something, and also that fashion is a lived practice, a way of being, that reaches far beyond appearances.

This understanding of fashion as a haptic experience, as an action, a way of being and indeed thinking, seems especially imperative at a moment when fashion is increasingly understood as a series of brief, fleeting spectacles. Fashion now is typically manifested in the form of a never-ending stream of visual experiences, a condition that becomes ever more apparent and ubiquitous with the advent and rapid development of digital technologies. This has led to a situation where an ever-greater amount of fashion, or at least its commonly accepted manifestation, clothing, is more than likely experienced virtually rather than in actuality. The rise of e-commerce and the recent proliferation of the immersive fashion exhibition being just two examples of the digitally enabled visual consumption of contemporary fashion.

Returning to the dictionary definitions, it is interesting to consider that the first recorded usage of many of them hail from what we might term the later Renaissance period, when the sense of sight accrued supremacy over the rest of the senses. At this time, sight was reformulated as the sense that imparts knowledge and equates to modern ideas of information, as opposed to earlier periods when the senses could be understood to be on a par with each other, constructing a sensorium, where the senses of touch, hearing, taste, and smell were as valuable in understanding our world as was the sense of sight. This shift in significance toward the visual, a situation that we are still very much in thrall to, occurred at a time when the notion of a culture of appearances also gained ascendancy, a culture in which clothing played a seminal role and assumed many of the functions we recognize it still fulfills today, in terms of confirming status, enforcing hierarchies, and representing social divisions both locally and globally. This segmentation was obviously due to increasingly sophisticated techniques of visual representation, where appearances were paramount, a situation that has continued in our current visual, media-saturated existence.

But fashion, if we focus strictly on clothing and textiles, appeals to senses other than the visual, most certainly touch and, as is called for in this book, the sonic. I am of course here referring to physical clothing rather than representations of clothing where sight reigns supreme and which have brought us to our current relationship with fashion as being overwhelmingly visual. Taking these dictionary definitions as possible indicators, we can begin to discern that Fashion Thinking must imply shaping, building, making thoughts and ideas, and crucially, that it must constantly strive to subvert, transform, frame, and adapt those same thoughts and ideas, as a restless, agitated, and irregular way of thinking.

My attempts at applying this process and the exploration that follows is necessarily in a nascent state and, like a garment, will continue to undergo a series of fittings and alterations until it becomes fit for purpose. My ambition for Fashion Thinking emerges from personal experiences when writing about fashion and textiles.

These experiences have been pleasurable, stimulating, and challenging, but in turn have always been accompanied by a sense that established conventions of academic writing fail to capture the wayward, all-inclusive, and indisciplinary processes of fashion implicit in the dictionary definitions considered above. This sense coupled with the practice of aligning fashion with, or through, other disciplinary lenses, which is prevalent in much fashion writing, again seems to me to limit fashion's scope and potential. Fashion itself flees from constraint and convention; it is never settled and content to follow a single direction, and neither should thinking and writing about fashion. Fashion Thinking demands plurality, breadth, and experimentation, and does not need the conceptual safety net within which a single disciplinary perspective aims to encompass it. To explore the possibilities of Fashion Thinking, it will therefore be necessary to identify some of those practices that define the creation of fashion itself, in order to test them as alternative ways of approaching a subject. These practices help us to understand fashion as a method, as making, as bringing into existence, and so, consequently, to understand Fashion Thinking itself as inspired by this very act of fashioning.

Fashion is neophilic

It is predicated on newness, on novelty. We expect fashion to be new, to be in opposition to what has gone before, to make what was previously newly fashionable, familiar, stale, even undesirable. This desire for the next, the swift disenchantment with the here and now, is that same process Walter Benjamin memorably characterized as taking the form of a love affair in which one needs to fall out of love with the previous object of desire in order to be able to fall in love again, in love anew. This association of fashion with newness has, of course, been a principal cause of its perceived superficiality, its fickleness and preoccupation with novelty. But there is an immediate tension to be discerned here, between the denigration of fashion as trivial and frivolous and the often-celebrated pursuit of originality. In particular, the advocacy of innovation and the innate attraction to what is different and unknown has been characterized as fueling creativity and invention in many other fields. Sustaining fashion's neophilia, however, is also its relationship to the concept of anticipation. Fashion's pursuit of the new necessarily triggers the stimulation of expectation, the state of longing for what is yet unknown and unseen, for the possibilities of what is to come, what can be imagined and anticipated, an eagerness for the unfamiliar. Fashion thrives on the yearning for, on the desire for, and on the imagining of itself.

Fashion is contrary

Closely aligned to its pursuit of the new, fashion functions in opposition, disobedience, and antagonism. Not merely to what has gone before, as in the newly "unfashionable," but operating in a condition of being constantly contrary to the norm, to the familiar, to the conventional. This contrary state functions irrespective of the object it contradicts, for both the everyday and the remarkable are subject to its antagonisms, dependent on which are in ascendancy. Fashion's relationship to distinction and conformity is symbiotic, and is played out in sartorial terms in the contest between the "classic" and the unconventional. Fashion is sustained by this dichotomy, in the collision of opposites generating the notion of style, the maintenance of design hierarchies, and the establishment of progression and development. Fashion's opposition requires the repetition of endless seasonal change endlessly repeated, with difference becoming cyclical. Recurrences and returns, variations of the same, provide the fabric that fashion embellishes with the rediscovered, the previously visited.

Fashion is transformative

Cloth is transformed into clothing; clothing transforms the wearer. Fashion's transformations are its narratives, chains of events, movements, progressions, and journeys. Sartorial translations are distilled in the runway show, a sequential progression, a procession, a ritual that both transforms and is transforming. Fashion journeys from one place to another, from one time to another, from one state to another, from one form to another. It thrives in a constant condition of transition, of displacement, and evoking Félix Guattari and Gilles Deleuze's celebrated concept, is in a constant state of *becoming* fashion, a restless condition charged with potential atomization and dispersal, as with ever-shifting flocks and swarms. Fashion oscillates around, contains and abandons the garment as swiftly as it moves to encompass the next, to absorb the wearer, the consumer, the creator, the spectator, the listener. Contact with fashion effects transformation, propels journeys, and induces encounters to come. It is a series of restless, unfixed, turbulent, unsettled incursions into the larger movement of fashion, that in turn becomes part of a slower entropic parade, approaching stasis until the journey recommences. Fashion is procedural, ceremonial, and ritualistic, a celebration of pauses, reruns, approaches, and retreats.

Fashion is heterotemporal

It continuously collapses the distance between past and present, between before and after, between gone and to come. It is uchronic and makes up what was, redressing history, embellishing antiquity, and idealizing the forthcoming. It overlaps time, condenses different temporalities, applies temporalities to space, thickening and condensing time, forming chronotopes of cloth, compressing, dissolving, and atomizing epochs and eras, recalibrating, regulating, and resetting time. Fashionable time is always reflexive and reflective, counting backward while counting down the moments until the next arrives. The compression of styles, references, eras, modes, and forms results in time that is familiar and recognizable, experienced via the partial, the incomplete, and the unexpected. Times are stitched together in order to be pulled apart, and chronologies interrogated, made submissive, and recalibrated. Fashion's temporalities wear thin, condense, and are constantly concluding in order to recommence. Fashion is late, early, and on time; fashion is too late, too early, and never on time; fashion is avant-garde and démodé.

Fashion is ludic

Play creates, inspires, and propagates fashion. Humor, irony, parody, absurdity, and illogicality are its most serious features. Play prevents fixity, counters stagnation, and sets the cycle in motion; it interrupts its inevitability and restarts it elsewhere. Fashion play is strategic, combative, confrontational, and resistant—in and out of fashion being the eternal game. It is formed from the accidental, the spontaneous, the coincidental. Misalignment, incongruity, the inappropriate, and the untimely offer unlimited possibilities, unlimited reinvention, unlimited reprisals, unlimited scope for fashionable play. The ludic is ultimately social, communicative, and discursive; its creativity lies in interactions, dialogue, and exchange. Its humor is often its greatest tool, with irony, mockery, and paradox lining its playful surfaces. Play valorizes, restores, and honors the disregarded, and as such, it is relentless in its arrogations. No borders are impervious to fashion's ludic strategies, no boundaries respected, no limits observed; all can be subverted, destabilized, and refashioned. Like play, fashion is social, communicative, therapeutic, frustrating, combative, and joyous. The communication of fashion often relies on the merest glance or movement without recourse to words, comprised of signs and gestures, gatherings and intimacies, winners and losers.

Fashion is magnetic

It attracts its constituencies, gathers and holds tight its fundamental structures. It persuades, beckons, and seduces. Promotion and consumption depend on fashion's fascination, its forceful allure, offering the promise of proximity, to be held tight to a center that flees as quickly as it is neared. An irresistible dynamism that pulls, draws, and charms those within its force fields, fashion simultaneously repels those resistant to its temptations. Fashion acts as a lodestone attracting not just its essential iron, the dressed body and its referents, but a panoply of stimuli, provocations, influences, associations, and effects that grows and is augmented incessantly, becoming its own fashion-inflected repository. So powerful are fashion's force fields that those beyond or at least at fashion's outer edges are nevertheless lured and seduced by its charms, finding in fashion the perfect metaphor, inspiring allegories, fables, and embodiments past and present. No matter, no substance, no property can resist its pull for long, and such resistance can only serve to increase fashion's extent.

Neophilic, contrary, transformative, heterotemporal, ludic, magnetic. Can these qualities help construct a methodology with which not just to approach the manifold operations and procedures of fashion and its systems but utilize those same qualities to strive toward alternative modes of inquiry, whether textual, visual, sonic, or performative? Many of the characteristics outlined above are to be found in other disciplines, in other activities, but Fashion Thinking advocates their use not only to explore the subject itself but also to interrogate its actual method of inquiry, to think fashionably. This is a process that cherishes contradiction, that contravenes borders, hierarchies, and chronologies, that is emotional and joyous, that flees the definitive and embraces the incomplete.

The Sound of
Fashion Thinking

What follows is a sample, one might say a toile, of what
Fashion Thinking might be in application. Like a toile,
it is a rough, a trial, a sketch that will invariably remain
incomplete, unfinished, and subject to alteration and
modifications. Like a toile, it is also a testing ground,
a form of thinking through ideas, a manifestation of
influences and possibilities that, after processes of
refinement, editing, and modification, leads to the finished
garment that will be presented, promoted, styled, and
possibly acquired and worn. However, unlike a toile,
which is usually consigned to the archive, if kept at all,
only to resurface when some of the ideas it encompasses
are to be rethought or reworked, this toile is revealed.
This intentionally exposes and exhibits those formative
processes, the thinkings and rethinkings, the failures and
successes, the shortenings and lengthenings, the takings
in and lettings out, the ambitions and desires. It is marked,
drawn on, tacked, sewn, and pinned. It displays the signs
and scars of its making, traces that in a conventional toile
must be hidden from view lest it shatter the expected
perfection of the finished garment. Here the workings-
out are in plain sight, and the fashionable sleight of
hand where garments appear fully formed, bearing little
or no traces of their production, is resisted. As with a
toile, this demonstration of Fashion Thinking may be
reworked and reimagined, pulled apart and started again,
adapted, modified, transformed, and from a single toile,
many varieties of garments can be trialed anew and are
possible. This toile provides a written template of the
possibilities of Fashion Thinking. Although it takes the

form of a text, an assemblage of words, Fashion Thinking as a methodology can just as appropriately be applied to other media, other outcomes. Similarly, I have chosen as its initial focus a product of the fashion system, the fashion exhibition, partly as a result of my own experience curating fashion, but it should be emphasized that Fashion Thinking does not demand that fashion be its subject.

The Sound of Fashion Thinking is an account of a fashion exhibition with no fashion, where our auditory responses to the few exhibits and the environments in which they are placed act as a series of calls to enter the spaces of Fashion Thinking. The aim of this "tour" of an imaginary exhibition is to engage audiences in a process of thinking about fashion, specifically its production and dissemination, sonically. The decision to prioritize sound and the sense of hearing reflects my own personal Fashion Thinking journey. Having written about fur, and understanding its primary attraction and how its sociocultural and emotional significance is achieved via the sense of touch, which I argue outweighs even its visual impact, I have become increasingly interested in thinking about how else we can experience and explore fashion beyond the visual. Therefore, following the tactile, the sonic experience of fashion has become for me increasingly insistent as an alternative way of thinking about fashion and exploring its potential. My experience as both a visitor and curator has increased my awareness of the impossible "silence" of the fashion exhibition, a silence at odds with fashion's noisy, persistent aural power encountered at all stages, from production and creation to consumption and wearing. Curating has also made me acutely aware of the exclusivity of the conventional fashion exhibition, which relies almost entirely on the sense of sight to see and read about the objects on display.

I feel this is an unsustainable situation that ignores many potential, differently abled visitors. Lastly, and at the risk of overpersonalizing this account of how I arrived at a fashion exhibition about sound, my own encounters with hearing loss, referred to in the text that follows, have made me acutely aware of the sonic potential of fashion, one that I contend demands attention. *The Sound of Fashion Thinking* therefore utilizes our sonic engagement with clothing and textiles as a means to explore a range of cultural, political, economic, and social concerns.

Recently, an increasing number of museums and art institutions have begun to include fashion-related exhibitions in their programs, an acknowledgment of the popularity of fashion as a subject with contemporary audiences. This has resulted in a seemingly endless stream of monographic designer shows that present garments, typically chronologically, in a celebration of the star designer as "genius." These spectacles consolidate the canon of the great and the good of fashion with little or no critical analysis of fashion as a system itself, nor of its wider impact and understanding. If not celebrating specific designers, other fashion exhibitions take a more thematic approach, and while this offers scope for a potentially more diverse range of objects, many of these tend to suffer from the same disciplinary—or, one might argue, interdisciplinary—constraints as have beset fashion writing and publishing. These exhibitions are invariably didactic, exhorting the visitor to "see" fashion in a particular way, and the garments themselves to conform to the institutional regulation of all museum objects, instantly "elevated" to something beyond mere clothing, their original function as worn garments stripped away and now constrained to "tell" whichever story the particular institution commands it to. *The*

Sound of Fashion Thinking would ask audiences to hear rather than see, and thereby provide a fresh understanding of what a fashion exhibition could be, and perhaps cannot be. While it might seem counterintuitive not to prioritize actual garments in a fashion exhibition, I believe that such an experience would encourage genuine interactivity with its audience and provide a catalyst for visitors to engage on alternative, personal, and critical levels with a subject that impacts every one of us.

The unrealized exhibition takes the form of a series of spaces through which the visitor/reader moves and experiences a series of immersive soundscapes. These soundscapes are summarized at the beginning of each room or space alongside a minimal indication of the various atmospheres of these spaces. The few objects on display are indicated in the text by adopting the conventional graphic layout of the museum object label. Beyond these nominal descriptions, the text itself deploys Fashion Thinking as a strategy to take the reader and imaginary visitor on a tour of the spaces, a series of scripted installations provoking further considerations on the possibilities of fashion, including a few of the many ways it can be encountered beyond the customary parade of lifeless garments that constitutes the majority of contemporary fashion exhibitions. The challenge presented by writing an account of an exhibition that does not exist, of a fashion exhibition that has no fashion, which is accompanied by no illustrations and attempts to put sound into words, is a means of testing the efficacy of Fashion Thinking as a methodology. To be unconstrained by having to describe clothing, and yet thinking about fashion expansively, and incorporating the characteristic operations intrinsic to the production and dissemination of fashion outlined above, could be understood as a similar call to that of Mitchell's exhortation for visual culture to address what lies outside of vision, in this case, to address fashion by what lies outside of the garment. *The Sound of Fashion Thinking* draws on the features, methods, and operations of fashion as a way of rethinking the possibilities of what a fashion exhibition might sound and feel like while simultaneously using those same methods to reconsider the process of writing fashion.

Repeated words, sounds, phrases, and references occur across and throughout the different spaces of *The Sound of Fashion Thinking*, an acknowledgment of the cyclical structure of fashion, not just its seasonal cycles but the processes of repetition, recurrence, revisitation, and referencing that are intrinsic to the design process itself. Sentences and phrases are often intentionally brief, even abrupt, as a way of recognizing how, when thinking about a subject, ideas, allusions, memories, and situations emerge instantaneously and arrive unexpectedly and unbidden. It is this process, equally essential to the creation of fashion itself, that this brevity of writing attempts to emulate and respect. The original thought is left unhampered and unfiltered by the conventions of academic referencing in the main text, although in the manner of a film, a list of credits is supplied. In opposition to this deployment of concision, other sentences are lengthy and sparingly punctuated, causing the reader to be conscious of the very act of reading, to become active and participatory in the decision as to where and when to draw breath. This involvement is a tribute not only to the essentially collaborative design process that is fundamental to the production of fashion but also to how the reader/consumer is the necessary final stage of any creative product, be that a garment, or in this case, a text.

Sounds, whether in the form of onomatopoeic imitations, reproductions of snatches of song lyrics, evocations of lengthier musical compositions, or the repeated use of certain words, terms, and phrases, either read or recited, instigate sonic rhythms and patterns distinct from any specific meaning. This desire to detain, if not fully capture, sound has been driven by the desire to reclaim for fashion a more complete sensate significance than its avowed visuality. Further, my own experience of the sense of hearing, as related in one of the autobiographical passages that punctuates the text, has been another incentive to utilize Fashion Thinking as a method to focus attention on how we might "think" through a subject, in this case, how we might "hear" a subject. This last endeavor is also responsible for one of the overriding sonic encounters of *The Sound of Fashion Thinking*. Repeated throughout the exhibition and tour is the sound of bells. The concepts of anticipation and expectation that structure fashion's neophilia are expressed by this repeated utilization of the bell. As an instrument of sound, but also understanding its function as an object that announces, the sound of a bell prepares and makes ready those who hear it. This sonic expectation introduced in the first space, *Bells*, is then heard throughout the proceeding spaces, developing, transitioning, and located in different structures, be they lyric, sonic, literary, or musical, but always with the intention of summoning and raising expectations, as does the presentation of fashion. Alongside the sound of bells, other sounds are continuously repeated, including those that attempt to describe the sound of fabrics, as in the second space, *Frou Frou*, the sound of manufacturing in *Production*, or the sound of cutting in the final space, *Bespeak*. The repetitions, always with variations, are deployed in order to emulate the constantly evolving understanding of fashion, its progressions

and regressions, its structuring and restructuring,
its resonance and echoes.

Accepted temporal progressions are dispensed within
The Sound of Fashion Thinking with material from distinct
and often remote temporalities brought together as a form
of atemporality or heterotemporality, reflecting fashion's
customary borrowing of references from different eras
and its collapsing of time, often on the one garment and
finally on the body of the wearer. There is also a sense in
the exhibition spaces that time is being reassembled and
fictionalized, a form of uchronia that is often apparent
in fashion, where the past and the future are constantly
reimagined and literally made up into clothing. Cross-
referencing other parts of the text, other spaces in
the exhibition, other devices and objects encountered
previously, is a textual device that acknowledges the
processes of variation, repetition, recall, referencing,
and memory that are essential to Fashion Thinking.

Certain eras in the text emerge more noticeably than
others—for example, the 1980s or the postwar period, a
paradigm for how fashion itself is utilized by subsequent
moments to typify and characterize previous eras, and
how often the surest method to evoke the past is through
dress. This explores fashion as chronotopic, where
the appearance of fashion, be that in actual garments,
images, music, or text, coalesce to form "fashion time,"
a time defined by fashion. But in this text, the collision
of multiple fashion times interrogates this operation
and suggests that fashion and its temporalities are
constantly shifting, mutable, and porous. Just as strict
chronologies are dispensed with, so too does *The Sound
of Fashion Thinking* resist hierarchies. Accessible material
collides with the arcane, the commonly recognized and

consumed with the exclusive and forgotten, a tribute to fashion's magnetism, its ability to attract, assemble, and present ideas, forms, and inspirations from vastly different sources. Fashion's unapologetic borrowing, assimilation, and forced alliances are echoed in the text's use of material both internal and external to the field of fashion studies itself.

The ludic drive apparent in so many areas of fashion production is present in the ironic tone assumed throughout *The Sound of Fashion Thinking*, in its awkwardness, in its fascination with the incongruous, and in formal devices such as the museum label to distinguish the exhibition objects from their sonic context. A number of questions, in turn rhetorical, hypothetical, passionate, or open-ended, are posed throughout the text. The intention of these interrogations is to act as a reminder that fashion is an inherently social, communicative, and dialogic process. The questions are a way of facilitating the engagement of the reader, to make the text personally relevant, to provide an opportunity for disagreement and for a pause in which to reflect and offer alternatives. For any text, whether written or in other forms, needs its reader/viewer to participate and, if not complete it, certainly to continue its ongoing transformation and development. What might be considered traditionally written passages utilizing conventional sentence structure and syntax, such as the descriptions of textiles in *Frou Frou*, or the details concerning acoustic neuromas in *Production*, acknowledge established literary conventions but, in their partiality and incompleteness, also acknowledge the limitations of such conventions. Similarly, the descriptions of the various garments presented in Viktor & Rolf's collection *Bells* (a catalyst for much of the Fashion Thinking deployed in the text) are written in the form of a pastiche of fashion journalism from the mid-twentieth century, a period where words were still valued as much as images to "speak" fashion. The autobiographical sequences retelling certain of my encounters with fashion are at times direct, at others more oblique, recognizing that any reader will bring their own experiences to a subject, and that in this instance, we all have access to our own personal fashion archive, comprised of memories of real garments, real experiences, received knowledge about fashion, mediated images, allusions, and much more. These autobiographical sections are "true" to a degree but, like all memories and like fashion itself, are subject to variation, remaking, and reinterpretation, as Robert Graves in his sonically saturated short story "The Shout" suggested: "'My story is true,' he said, 'every word of it. Or, when I say that my story is "true," I mean at least that I am telling it in a new way. It is always the same story, but I sometimes vary the climax and even recast the characters. Variation keeps it fresh and therefore true. If I were always to use the same formula, it would soon drag and become false.'"

Many of the references to specific garments, designers, music, songs, and snatches of lyrics that erupt across *The Sound of Fashion Thinking* emerged as sudden recollections during the process of Fashion Thinking embarked on while writing this book. These are included not with the intention of constructing new hierarchies, fashionable or otherwise, for all are of equal value, but in the belief that these memories, these reminiscences, these immediate comparisons need to be listened to. What might be understood as personal "playlists" and individual "wardrobes" must be replayed, reopened and contribute uncensored and unedited when Fashion Thinking. This must be done with the same lack of restraint that a designer enjoys when working with cloth, allowing for its weight, its ability to fall and drape in unexpected ways, to influence the eventual garment and how it will be worn. On a structural level, the admittance of these autobiographical passages and individual memories not only disrupts any emerging narratives or chronology, but also questions notions of validity, authenticity, and accuracy. *The Sound of Fashion Thinking* strenuously avoids the hazard of replacing one grand narrative with another, instead offering up and treating with equal worth partial, disparate, and incomplete narratives, sets of possibilities, sonic snapshots and stills. While these are necessarily presented in sequence, their repetition, juxtaposition, disappearance, and reemergence indicate how this same text, as with the analogy of refashioned cloth, can be reformatted, reheard, and repositioned, to create further narratives, to sustain a mode of relentless inquiry, refusal, and potentiality.

Evoking the idea of the still, normally associated with film, and before visiting the "exhibition," *The Sound of Fashion Thinking*'s cast is supplied in order of appearance. Much of this content will be familiar to the reader, but it is provided, in addition to the closing final credits referred to above, with the intention of reinforcing the diversity and inclusivity that is another key attribute of Fashion Thinking. The accumulation of names, ideas, and sounds function, as do the early processes of fashion design, when different materials and inspiration gathered from disparate arenas are assembled to create the "feel" of a collection. This same idea of assemblage grows throughout the text with sounds and references building, growing, overlapping, and repeating, so that by the exhibition's end, the visitor has experienced an encounter with Fashion Thinking that is, like the sound of bells that reverberates throughout its spaces, insistent, summoning, and expectant. *The Sound of Fashion Thinking* is an experiment, a toile, an investigation to test whether we can think about fashion differently, and in turn, use the way fashion is thought into existence to consider other questions, other subjects. Neophilia, contrariness, transformation, heterotemporality, the ludic, and the magnetic not only make fashion but speak of its seductions, its frustrations, its necessity, and its universality. When listening to fashion's voice, to the sounds and noises it makes, we can also hear how to think with all of our senses, an action expressive of the desire for inclusivity, potential, and liberation, which is fundamental to the process of Fashion Thinking itself.

CAST

in order of appearance

BELLS

HUGO

Victor Hugo, 1802–85
Novelist, poet, playwright, politician,
and exile. Conductor of séances and
producer of automatic drawings.
Author of *Notre-Dame de Paris*
(*The Hunchback of Notre Dame*), 1831

LAUGHTON

Charles Laughton, 1899–1962
Actor. Played Quasimodo, the deaf,
hunchbacked bell ringer of Notre-Dame
Cathedral in *The Hunchback of Notre-Dame*,
directed by William Dieterle, 1939

VIKTOR & ROLF

Viktor Horsting and Rolf Snoeren
Fashion designers

OJIBWA

Anishinaabe people known by several
names, including Ojibway or Chippewa.
Their homeland covers much of the Great
Lakes region and the northern plains of the US.
Ojibwa believe that spiritual power moves
through the air and that the sound
of jingle dresses forms part of a
sonic healing process

WALTER

Walter Benjamin, 1892–1940
Philosopher and cultural critic.
Among the writings assembled in his
unfinished *Das Passagen-Werk*
(*The Arcades Project*), begun in 1927,
are his thoughts on the importance,
and cyclical structure, of fashion

MISS SHELDRAKE

During the 1960s maintained the
choristers' robes and priests' vestments
for St. Thomas of Canterbury Church,
Brentwood, Essex

BOJANGLES

Bill "Bojangles" Robinson, 1878–1949
Tap dancer, actor, and singer. Famous for his
rhythmically complex step sequences,
including his celebrated
"staircase" routine

EDGAR

Edgar Allan Poe, 1809–49
Poet, writer, and literary critic. Author of
The Bells, a heavily onomatopoeic poem notable
for its diacopic use of the word "bells,"
published posthumously in 1849

PHYLLIS NELSON

1950–98
American singer.
Most famous for her 1985 hit "Move Closer"

ARTFUL DODGER

Character in Charles Dickens's
Oliver Twist, 1837–39. Real name Jack Dawkins.
Pickpocket. Leader of child criminal gang

PEARLIES

Pearly Kings and Queens.
Members of the organized London charitable
tradition celebrated for wearing clothes decorated
with mother-of-pearl buttons. This custom follows
the tradition of nineteenth-century costermongers,
or street traders, who decorated the seams
of their trousers with pearl buttons

EUROPA

Phoenician princess abducted by Zeus in the
shape of a bull. Mother of King Minos of Crete.
Continent of Europe named after her

NANA

Lily Maude Wallis, née Southgate, 1891–1967
Author's maternal grandmother

MR. BAUDELAIRE/CHARLES

Charles Baudelaire, 1821–67
Poet, essayist, and art critic. Admirer of Poe.
Philosopher of dandyism

HERR POELL/CCP

Carol Christian Poell
Fashion designer

MENEER MARGIELA

Martin Margiela
Fashion designer

ELSA

Elsa Schiaparelli, 1890–1973
Fashion designer

LESAGE

François Lesage, son of Albert Lesage and
Marie-Louise Favot. Dynasty of highly skilled
embroiderers. Founded Maison Lesage, the oldest
Parisian embroidery atelier, which worked with
the most celebrated designers of twentieth-century
haute couture. In 2002, Lesage became part of
Chanel's subsidiary Paraffection, a collective of
fashion-related specialist craft workshops

FATH

Jacques Fath, 1912–54
Fashion designer

DIOR

Christian Dior, 1905–57
Fashion designer

MCQUEEN/
JACK THE RIPPER LEE

Lee Alexander McQueen, 1969–2010
Fashion designer

BJÖRK

Björk Guðmundsdóttir
Singer, composer, and actor. Known for
her three-octave vocal range

WRIGHTON

Gareth Wrighton
Fashion designer and art director

NICK KNIGHT

Fashion photographer and founder
of SHOWstudio.com

THOM BROWNE

Fashion designer

MRS. DALLOWAY

Clarissa Dalloway
Character in Virginia Woolf's novel
Mrs. Dalloway, 1925

PETER LEWIS-CROWN/PETER

1930–2024
Couturier, teacher, director,
and subsequently last owner of
the House of Lachasse

BERNARD HERRMANN

1911–75
Composer and conductor.
Known for his film scores, most notably his
collaborations with Alfred Hitchcock

IAIN

Iain R. Webb
Award-winning fashion writer,
curator, and teacher

BLITZ KIDS

Habitués of the Tuesday club night in the
late 1970s and early '80s at Blitz, Covent Garden,
London. Credited with originating the
New Romantic subculture

OLDFIELD

Mike Oldfield
Musician, songwriter, and composer.
Best known for his 1973 debut
studio album *Tubular Bells*

RAVEL/MAURICE

Maurice Ravel, 1875–1937
Composer, pianist, and conductor.
Admirer of Poe. Collector of automata.
Composer of "La vallée des cloches" ("The Valley
of Bells"), 1904–5, a piano work imitating the
sounds of bells heard ringing in a
mechanical landscape

GRAINGER

Percy Grainger, 1882–1961
Composer, arranger, and pianist

DEBUSSY

Claude Debussy, 1862–1918
Composer. Regarded as the first
impressionist composer, although he
rejected the term. Wrote *La cathédrale engloutie*
(*The Sunken Cathedral*), a 1910 piano work inspired
by the legend of a submerged cathedral off the
coast of the mythical island of Ys in Brittany,
which on clear mornings rises, and the
sounds of bells, chanting, and
organ music can be heard

VIRGINIA

Miss Virginia of Lachasse
Wood, plaster, and wax miniature mannequin
based on Lachasse's leading house model,
Miss Virginia Woodford. Made in the mid-1950s,
the doll's wardrobe was created by Owen, then-
creative director of the House, and included
accessories from the leading London
manufacturers of the period

MS. KASS

Carmen Kass
Model. President of the Estonian chess federation
from 2004 to 2011. Noted for her distinctive walk.
In 2024 Kass, visibly pregnant, walked for
the s/s 2025 Vetements collection

FROU FROU

PRIKKER

Johan Thorn Prikker, 1868–1932
Symbolist painter. Architect and interior designer.
Associate of the art group Les XX and the
Salon de la Rose+Croix

BARTHES

Roland Barthes, 1915–80
Literary theorist, philosopher, and semiotician.
Author of *Système de la mode* (*The Fashion
System*), 1967, and, among many other articles
on fashion-related subjects, the essay
"Dandyism and Fashion," 1962

SADE

Helen Folasade Adu
Singer. Lead vocalist of the band Sade.
First Nigerian-born artist to
win a Grammy award

CHRISTO

Christo Vladimirov Javacheff, 1935–2020
Artist couple with Jeanne-Claude Denat de
Guillebon, 1935–2009. Most noted for large-scale,
site-specific, wrapped installations

VINCENT KORDA

1897–1979
Art director

WORMS

Fictional couturier in Émile Zola's novel
La curée (*The Kill*)

WORTH

Charles Frederick Worth, 1825–95
Fashion designer. Founder of the
House of Worth. Popularly credited
as the father of haute couture

ZOLA

Émile Zola, 1840–1902
Novelist, playwright, and journalist.
Advocate of political liberalism. He wrote every
day, taking the Latin phrase *Nulla dies sine linea*—
"Not a day without a line"—as his maxim

GANDHI

Mohandas Karamchand Gandhi, popularly
known as Mahatma Gandhi, 1869–1948
Lawyer, political ethicist, and advocate of
nonviolent resistance. Led the campaign for Indian
independence. Campaigned that Indians should wear
khadi (homespun cloth) as opposed to British textiles,
and that all Indian people, regardless of class,
should spend time each day at a spinning
wheel in the move toward
independence

JAINS

Followers of Jainism, an ancient Indian religion.
Jain philosophy encompasses belief in reincarnation
and advocates *ahimsa*, or nonviolence,
and that no living being, however small,
should be harmed or killed

SCHEELE

Carl Wilhelm Scheele, 1742–86
Pharmaceutical chemist. Inventor of toxic,
bright green artificial dye obtained by heating
sodium carbonate and adding
arsenious oxide

MS. WILSON

Elizabeth Wilson
Researcher, writer, and pioneering feminist.
Wrote the seminal fashion theory text
*Adorned in Dreams: Fashion
and Modernity* in 1985

MS. TAYLOR

Lou Taylor
Pioneering dress historian,
teacher, and curator

MÜNCHHAUSEN

Baron Munchausen
Fictional character created by the writer
Rudolf Erich Raspe in his 1785 book
*Baron Munchausen's Narrative
of His Marvelous Travels and
Campaigns in Russia*

VOLKER EICHELMANN

Artist, curator, and teacher

ROLAND RUST

Artist, solutions architect, and
enabler of all things digital

CAPTAIN PETER LEKEUX

1649–1723
Prominent master silk weaver.
One of the ten wealthiest Huguenots in England

ANNA MARIA GARTHWAITE

1688–1763
Preeminent English textile designer.
Created distinctive, vivid floral designs
for the Spitalfields silk industry

HUGUENOTS

Persecuted French protestants,
many of whom emigrated to England in the
late seventeenth and eighteenth centuries

WALLOONS

Predominantly French-speaking residents
of the Walloon area of southern Belgium

REVEREND EPHRAIM AND MOTHER REJOYCE

Parents of Anna Maria Garthwaite

HOGARTH

William Hogarth, 1697–1764
Painter, engraver, social satirist, and art
and design theorist. Published his
Analysis of Beauty in 1753

GIBSON GIRLS

Personification of fin de siècle
American beauty as depicted in the drawings of
illustrator Charles Dana Gibson. The Gibson Girl
had an exaggerated S-shaped torso achieved
by wearing a swan-bill corset

MAURICE AND VERDINE

Maurice White, 1941–2016
Singer and composer

Verdine White
Bassist

Founding members of the band
Earth, Wind & Fire

VICAR OF WAKEFIELD

Central character in Oliver Goldsmith's
1766 novel *The Vicar of Wakefield:
A Tale, Supposed to Be Written by Himself*

DUCHAMP

Marcel Duchamp, 1887–1968
Painter, sculptor, and writer

SERRES

Michel Serres, 1930–2019
Philosopher, theorist, and writer.
Author of *Les cinq sens: Philosophie des
corps mêlés* (*The Five Senses: A Philosophy
of Mingled Bodies*), 1985

TRANE

John Coltrane, 1926–67
Saxophonist, composer, and bandleader.
At the forefront of the free jazz movement
and pioneer of modal jazz

HENRI MEILHAC AND
LUDOVIC HALÉVY

Henri Meilhac, 1831–97
Dramatist and librettist

Ludovic Halévy, 1834–1908
Novelist and librettist

Collaborated on Georges Bizet's opera
Carmen, 1875; Jules Massenet's opera
Manon, 1884; and the play *Frou Frou*, 1869

RENOUVIER

Charles Renouvier, 1815–1903
Philosopher

PRODUCTION

VICTOR BURGIN

Conceptual artist and writer

GRACIE

Gracie Fields, 1898–1979
Actor, singer, and comedian. Known as "'Our Gracie"
and "The Lancashire Lass." Early in her career, as
her success in the music hall grew, she gave up
her job in a Lancashire cotton mill

RUSSOLO

Luigi Russolo, 1885–1947
Futurist painter, composer, and constructor
of experimental musical instruments

PIATTI

Ugo Piatti, 1888–1953
Painter and instrument maker

SYLVESTER

1947–88
Singer and composer. Known for his distinct falsetto
voice, a string of disco hits in the late 1970s and '80s,
and his flamboyant and groundbreaking appearance,
wearing both male and female clothing

CRISTÓBAL BALENCIAGA

1895-1972
Fashion designer

ANDRÉ COURRÈGES

1923-2016
Fashion designer

PROUST

Marcel Proust, 1871-1922
Novelist, literary critic, and essayist

PACO RABANNE

1934-2023
Jeweler, fashion designer, and author

EMANUEL UNGARO

1933-2019
Fashion designer

STEICHEN

Edward Steichen, 1879-1973
Pioneering fashion photographer,
artist, and curator

BEATON

Cecil Beaton, 1904-80
Portrait and fashion photographer,
costume and set designer, and diarist

ALIX

Madame Grès, 1903–93
Fashion designer

LELONG

Lucien Lelong, 1889–1958
Fashion designer

ROCHAS

Marcel Rochas, 1902–55
Fashion designer

COLE

Cole Porter, 1891–1964
Composer and songwriter

MAD HATTER

Stephen Jones
Milliner and curator

GALLIANO

John Galliano
Fashion designer

MS. HAWES

Elizabeth Hawes, 1903–71
Fashion designer, political activist,
union organizer, and advocate
of gender equality

THEODOR SCHWANN

1810–82
Physician and physiologist

MERLIN

Mythical sorcerer featured in the legend
of King Arthur. Small species of falcon

DISNEY

Walt Disney, 1901–66
Animator, producer, and entrepreneur

STERLING HOLLOWAY

1905–92
Actor and voice of many Disney
cartoon characters

RUDYARD

Rudyard Kipling, 1865–1936
Novelist, poet, and journalist

KAA

Fictional python. Character in Kipling's
The Jungle Book, 1894

BERNARD NEWMAN

1903–66
Head designer for Bergdorf Goodman
department store and head costume
designer for RKO Pictures

ADRIAN

Adrian Adolph Greenberg, 1903–59
Fashion and costume designer for
Metro-Goldwyn-Mayer

IRENE

Irene Maud Lentz, 1901–62
Fashion and costume designer

TRAVILLA

William Travilla, 1920–90
Costume designer

EDITH HEAD

1897–1981
Costume designer

HELEN ROSE

1904–85
Costume and fashion designer

MONSIEUR SAILLARD

Olivier Saillard
Fashion curator and historian

COMME DES GARÇONS

Fashion label founded by
Rei Kawakubo

FRED

Fred Astaire, 1899–1987
Dancer, actor, and choreographer.
HUCK HAINES in *Roberta*, 1935

GINGER

Ginger Rogers, 1911–95
Actor and dancer.
COMTESSE SCHARWENKA
in *Roberta*

JANE

Jane Wyman, 1917–2007
Actor. LUCY GALLANT in
Lucy Gallant, 1955

CHARLTON

Charlton Heston, 1923–2008
Actor

MRS. DANVERS

Character in Daphne Du Maurier's
novel *Rebecca*, 1938

LAUREN

Lauren Bacall, 1924–2014
Actor. SCHATZE in
How to Marry a Millionaire, 1953

BETTY

Betty Grable, 1916–73
Actor and dancer. LOCO in *How to
Marry a Millionaire*

MARILYN

Marilyn Monroe, 1926–62
Actor and model. POLA in *How to
Marry a Millionaire*

ROBERTA/STEPHANIE

Characters in *Roberta*

NORMA

Norma Shearer, 1902–83
Actor

ROSALIND

Rosalind Russell, 1907–76
Actor

JOAN

Joan Crawford, ca.1906–77
Actor. CRYSTAL ALLEN in
The Women, 1939

MR. ALLAN SHIVERS

1907–85
Governor of Texas, 1949–57

RANDOLPH

Randolph Scott, 1898–1987
Actor. JOHN KENT in *Roberta*

TOM

Character in *How to Marry
a Millionaire*

MAXIM

Maxim de Winter
Character in *Rebecca*

DEMNA

Demna Gvasalia
Cofounder of Vetements and
creative director of Balenciaga

MARY HABBERFIELD

1915–2011
Sound editor and producer

JACK PARNELL

1923–2010
Drummer, composer,
and bandleader

MAX BOY

Nom de plume of the author of
Modes & Mannequins, 1946

MOLYNEUX

Captain Edward Molyneux, 1891–1974
Fashion designer

HARTNELL

Norman Hartnell, 1901–79
Fashion designer

BESPEAK

WILKINSON & SON

Thomas Wilkinson, 1782–1863
Premier Sheffield scissor manufacturer.
1840 "manufacturers to Her Majesty and Prince
Albert of fine scissors, shears, nail nippers, etc.,
and cutlery, silver plate, and dealers." Made
master cutler in 1843. Joined in the business
by his son George, 1814–1868

OGDEN NASH

1902–71
Poet. Famous for comic verse employing
unconventional rhyming schemes

KURT

Kurt Weill, 1900–1950
Composer. Collaborated with Bertolt Brecht

LOTTE

Lotte Lenya, 1898–1981
Singer and actor

KURT & LOTTIE

Author's dogs

REUBEN SYTNER

1887–1983
Tailor, lecturer, and author of
The Art of Fitting Gentlemen's Garments, 1955

THE OLD CONTEMPTIBLES

Nickname for the BEF (British Expeditionary Force),
the six divisions of the British army sent to the
Western Front during the First World War

QUEEN VICTORIA

1819–1901
British Queen
Reigned from 1837 to 1901

BEN SHERMAN

Arthur Benjamin Sugarman, 1925–87
Launched the first Ben Sherman shirt in 1963.
Influenced by classic American Ivy League shirts,
with the addition of a back hook and center-back
collar button, it was an immediate success

DAVID LONDON

Tailor

GILBERT & GEORGE

Gilbert Prousch (sometimes Proesch)
and George Passmore
Collaborative performance art duo and producers
of large-scale photography-based artworks

SEAN CONNERY

1930–2020
Actor. First actor to play James Bond
on-screen, starring in seven Bond films
between 1962 and 1983

JAMES BOND

Fictional secret service agent created
by Ian Fleming in 1953

BUFFALO

Buffalo Bill / Jame Gumb
Fictional serial killer created by Thomas Harris
in the 1988 novel *The Silence of the Lambs*

FRANKENSTEIN

Victor Frankenstein
Fictional scientist created by Mary Shelley
in her novel *Frankenstein; or, The
Modern Prometheus*, 1818

GEIN

Ed Gein, 1906–84
Convicted murderer and suspected
serial killer and body snatcher

ALEXIS CARREL

1873–1944
Surgeon, biologist, and eugenicist

SHELLEY

Mary Wollstonecraft Shelley, 1797–1851
Novelist

KARLOFF

Boris Karloff, born William Henry Pratt, 1887–1969
Actor and horror film icon, most notably
playing the creature in James Whale's
1931 film *Frankenstein*

WALTER SCOTT

1771–1832
Novelist and poet

SHAKESPEARE

William Shakespeare, 1564–1616
Playwright and poet

DOROTHY L. SAYERS

1893–1957
Crime novelist and playwright

ROSE HETTIE

Rose Hettie Laing, née Moore, 1918–94
Tailor, machinist, and designer.
Author's mother-in-law

DEKKER

Thomas Dekker, 1572–1632
Playwright and pamphleteer

ST. AGATHA OF SICILY

ca. 231–ca. 251
Christian saint and virgin martyr

MARQUIS

Marquis de Sade, 1740–1818
Writer, libertine, and political activist

ATROPOS

Eldest of the mythological Three Fates,
or Moirai, who cuts the thread of life.
Translates as "the inflexible"

SWANN

Charles Alexander Swann, character in
the 1954 film *Dial M for Murder*,
directed by Alfred Hitchcock

MARGOT

Margot Wendice, character in
Dial M for Murder

DELL

Dellores Marco Laing
Writer, lecturer, performer, and DJ.
Author's wife

FREUD

Sigmund Freud, 1856–1939
Neurologist and writer. Founder of psychoanalysis

ACTION MAN

Action figure launched in Britian
by Palitoy in 1966

MAX ERNST

1891–1976
Painter, collagist, sculptor,
and pioneer of the Dada movement

LYOTARD

Jean-François Lyotard, 1924–98
Philosopher, sociologist, and literary critic

KRISTEVA

Julia Kristeva
Philosopher, psychoanalyst,
feminist, and novelist

BAUDRILLARD

Jean Baudrillard, 1929–2007
Sociologist, philosopher, and media analyst

REI KAWAKUBO

Fashion designer and founder
of the label Comme des Garçons

LADY DI

Diana, Princess of Wales, 1961–97

CAROL

Carol McKay
Lecturer, curator, and museologist

JAMIE, BARBARA, AND VICTOR

Jamie Stapleton

Barbara Jax

Victor Rodriguez

Colleagues of the author,
MA Twentieth-Century Art Theory and History
degree course, Goldsmiths College,
University of London

JONATHAN SWIFT

1667–1745
Writer and satirist. Works include *A Tale
of a Tub*, 1704, which takes three inherited
coats as its central metaphor

VAL LEWTON

1904–51
Novelist, producer, and screenwriter

WARDEN SIMMS

Character in the film *Bedlam*, 1946

FREDDIE FRANCIS

1917–2007
Cinematographer and filmmaker

GEORGE CARTER

Character in the film
Tales from the Crypt, 1972

MAJOR WILLIAM ROGERS

Character in *Tales from the Crypt*

Bells

The space is filled with fog / dry ice. Spotlit and emerging from the fog is a projection of a still image from Viktor & Rolf's a/w 2000 *Bells* haute couture collection, of a model barely discernible on a fog-filled runway. Three vitrines, one containing a bronze bell head from Lower Niger, one an Ojibwa jingle dress, and the third, four small framed images of Edgar Allen Poe, Charles Baudelaire, Maurice Ravel, and Peter Lewis-Crown, respectively, are also spotlit. Soundscape: bells, change ringing, accounts from people who attended the Viktor & Rolf show, Ravel's "La vallée des cloches."

Hear the bells.

Their ringing, their chiming, their striking, their clanging,
their booming, their pealing, their roaring, their resonating,
their tolling, their clanging, their knelling, their sounding,
their resounding.

So many words to describe the sound.
So deficient.
So not sonorous.

Bells summon, bells warn, bells excite, bells prevent,
bells conjure, bells purify, bells block, bells circumscribe,
bells signal, bells delineate, bells define, bells alert,
bells evoke, bells compel, bells heal.

So many words to describe their properties. So wanting.
So not all-embracing.

Hell's bells.

> The bells! The bells! They
> made me deaf, you know.
>
> Hugo never wrote it.
> Laughton never said it.

Instead:

> *"his coat, half red, half purple,*
> *sprinkled with silver bells"*

That's more like it.
Bells and fashion.

Announcements. Expectations. Foretellings. Revelations.
Sanctifications. Elevations.

All this going to be. Going to happen. Going to excite.
Something's coming. Nearly here but not quite. Almost.

Fashion is summoned. Sanctified.
Warned against and warded off.
Anticipated, ordered, regulated, silenced,
mourned, celebrated. Beckoned.

Summoned by Bells

I am summoned by fashion.
What it might, could, must mean.
While what it is stales.

Exciting, only momentarily.
Is most effective when thinking what's not here
in stitch, cut, and style.
What could be.

Fetch me the next. Fetched. But what next?
Anticipated. Becoming but not being.
Fetch me another but different.
Send not to know.

Bells

Still image from Viktor & Rolf a/w 2000
haute couture collection

Presented July 17, 2000, Paris

A room filled with fog. Front row on either side of center runway murkily discernible, only washed-out salmon pink trousers bottom left register. Receding center spotlights catch and silhouette the approach of each model. No music. Noise of expectant crowd. Footsteps accompanied by the jingle of bells approach, get rhythmically louder. Grainy silhouette of model against backlight, no detail yet appears through the smoke. Crowd sounds of exclamation, cheering, chattering, clapping rise and fall, betraying anxiety, expectation, satisfaction, frustration.

> *"Bonjour, mesdames, mademoiselles.*
> *It gives me great pleasure to be your*
> *cicerone on our adventurous little*
> *voyage into Fashionland."*

First   Richest cream satin ... Gold top? Falls below the knee as a sonorous trench coat, tie belted, tie belled. Glossy richness nestling a banquet's worth of tinkling bells. Its upturned collar standing to attention as it listens to the sweet music it makes. Lined with a Christmas tree's worth of baby brass bells. Brazen baby, brash baby, bell baby bell. Palest cheeks reflect the burnished brassiness, such loud dressing! Surprising turn reveals back yoke stuffed with more bells. Brassy back fit to bursting, stuffed with sound, chock-full of chimes. A jangling cascade spills out from meticulously stitched hem, peek-a-bell. This resounding trench is no film noir disguise but entrances with its femme fatale resonance. Wear to be heard. Beware to beheard.

Second Clamor-inducing bell sleeves for this season's most arresting coat. Waffled wool defines a low-belted robe. Oversized shawl—more like a king-size beauty queen sash—collar meets at the hips with not much more below. Hybrid smoking jacket/bathrobe/tailored traveling rug is worn over nothing. White wool and pale flesh minimalism makes way for the big sonic surprise. Bounteous kimono sleeves are overcrowded with bells. Gleaming multitudes cascade. Bells abundant, bells beneficent, bells blooming and booming form brassy clusters of tinkling brazen grapes. Cornucopias of fruit ringings, belled bunches of shiny succulence. Taste their tinkling, relish their ringing, savor their sounding. But be warned, this brassy Bacchus wrap requires wrists of steel for full melodic effect.

Nervous applause is
summoned.

Ringing anticipates the appearance
actualized by rituals of ringing.
Made to be rung and to ring.
To summon and gather.
To disturb and repel. To warn and inform.
Worn to protect from witches.

To chime and time ceremonial movement.
The performance of becoming. The procession of fashion.

Worn to heal and restore.

Jingle dress

Ojibwa maker, ca. 1935

Conical bells made from the curled lids of tobacco tins, synthetic
fabric, cotton, plastic buttons, sequins, and rhinestones

Therapeutic jingling.
Bells for healing as foretold in his dream.

Dress the sick child in her jingle jangles. (Paleface flu)
Take her to the powwow. (Outlawed)
Make her dance. (Forbidden)
To the beat of the drum. (Proscribed)
Keep her feet close to the ground.
No backwardness. No circularity. No crossing of legs.
Such proscriptive medicine. Man.
Just the jangling and the beat of the drum.

"Like the beat beat beat
of the tom-tom"

Copper and silver cones made from the lids
of tobacco tins and coins and thimbles.
Severed to cease assimilation.
Sheared to reject conjugation.

Snipped to resist subjugation.
Cut to endow.
Snipped to bestow and hand-rolled to funnel magic.
Assembled and stitched.
Bound and lashed to make the sonic suit.
The body now a sounding instrument in harmony
with the drum. (Sick no longer)

> *"Only you beneath the moon*
> *and under the sun"*

Fashion is ceremonial, fashion heals, fashion is ritual,
fashion is radical, fashion returns.

Eternally returning and tiger's leaping.

Thanks a lot, Walter.

'80s revival and look what's happened.

Fashion as protest and fashion as remedy.
Jingling to drive away pandemics.
Jingling to disrupt and confuse.
Jingling at Standing Rock.
Jingling that is Idle No More.

> *"Here, 'twixt the church tower and the chapel spire*
> *Rang sad and deep the bells of my desire."*

As a choirboy my cotta, cassock and ruff would be newly starched and laundered by Miss Sheldrake for high days and holidays Easter, Whitsun, Advent. I remember the thrill of forcing apart the stuck-together, crackling sleeves, my hand separating the stiffness, where no hand had gone before, as 9:45 bells announced and beckon to Sunday sung Mass. The memory of pushing my probing fingers into the fortified, dazzling white cotton contrasting against the blue of my cassock is still vivid. I've often tried to think of what name describes that unpleasant shade of blue. Royal, azure, Cambridge? None of these; instead, it remains a color that for me says choir. The blue and the white a form of what would later be known in fashion parlance as color blocking, I suppose, choral chromatics if you want to be fancy. Chorister babble in the vestry as I hang up my external, secular clothing in the tall shallow cupboards, vague spicy aroma of incense lingering and mingling with peppery, musty, sweaty blend of old church, young boy and dirt, I can smell it now. My cassock was fastened by small, equally blue, cross-hatched buttons. 33 on an adult cassock marking Christ's years, but not so many as I recall on mine, worn from the ages of 6 to 11 when my voice started to break and I was unable to control the sudden whoopings and swoopings that ruptured my angelic treble. These buttons were held in place (and removed) by pins pushed through their small but perfectly formed shanks. No simple sewing here, elaboration deployed whenever possible, as with the services and rituals at which I sang. Altar gongs ringing three times, marking something inexplicable, insubstantial, transubstantial going on. But I guess this form of fastening was also practical as it allowed the buttons to be removed and replaced with ease when the cassock was cleaned. And the ruff, similarly starched, its perfect little cartridge pleats, not doubled and sewn like a Tudor ruff, but a looser ring (three times) of little starched tubes. A wee, covered button secured by corded loop assured a perfect fitting, circling my neck ready for the beatific decapitation. "Oh! He looks so angelic!" All of this every Sunday, morning and evening, and Saturdays too if weddings and, rarer, sung funerals required me and my mates' chanting. Rising from chorister to deputy to head, my look was accessorized by medals strung with pale blue, dark blue and red ribbons of corresponding thickness, the clanging of which sounded as they swung and hit the choir stalls, in the theater of peals, rings and chimes. Every Wednesday, Sunday and some Saturdays religion was my fashion, and I became a fashioned sonorous body.

Third   Viktor & Rolf's white bell-bottoms and chime-collared silk gazar shirt are kept in tune by a pitch-perfect, pin-tucked cummerbund. Silver and brass sleigh and tubular bells swing and ring free from trouser side seams. Sound marks construction, chimes define and tailor. Whistle while you work and jingle while you walk, it's off to pose we go! Belled seams and bells seem the perfect trimming for the modish Bojangles, the modern-day Mr. Robinson. What sonorous sashays sing as you swing in these melodious strides. Next, the bell-heavy collar is played out in the back section as a resounding cowl neck. Backing bells providing just the right register as you make your dissonant exit, your leitmotif of knells and peals the signal for ensemble head-turning.

More applause, please!

Fourth   City bells, got to be St. Martins, ring out both day and night to mark the arrival of this melodious whistle. Much more than five farthings' worth of immaculate chalk-stripe tailoring created this euphonious suit, a breathtaking bell-buttoned two-piece. A formal tintinnabulation of bells, both sleigh and crotal, weigh down and define its percussive collar and breast-skimming revers. Sharp tailoring like this needs celebration, and what better way to honor such musical sleight of hand than with batteries of bells? Each strut demands attention, each entrance achieving maximum impact. The second movement is heralded by more bells from the percussion section as jangle-slit cuffs announce absent turn ups. Whether dancing or fighting, these ghungroos—that's ankle bells to you—will make sure your high kicks and head kicks won't go unnoticed, and envy will be the order of the day when donning these tuneful threads.

Fashion is fed by anticipation. Fashion transforms what was into what will be. Fashion repeats anew.

Fashion interrogates redundancy.

Fashion supposes, fashion is speculative,
fashion converts, fashion is ritual, fashion is summoned,
fashion is neophilic, fashion is difference,
fashion beckons.

Fashion's ritual of the runway.

Promotion is predicated on anticipation.
Making space for the next whilst atomizing the previous.

The seasonal, the launch, the showcase, the pre-collection,
the first glimpse, the preview.

Fashion's belling deafens us to what has gone before.
Now the only sound is of imminent arrival.
Of foretelling. Of becoming material.
Chimes coalescing. Taking on form:

> *"How it swells!*
> *How it dwells*
> *On the Future! how it tells*
> *Of the rapture that impels*
> *To the swinging and the ringing*
> *Of the bells, bells, bells,*
> *Of the bells, bells, bells, bells,*
> *Bells, bells, bells—*
> *To the rhyming and the chiming of the bells!"*

Roger Edgar. Over and out.

Footsteps on marble. Or on wood or rubber.
Or on industrial gray floor paint.
Different sounds but all an act of striking. Idiophonic.

Bells already?

First room. Low murmur. Anyone there?

> *"Cooee! Cooee! Mr. Shifter. Light refreshment* [...]
> *Do you know the piano's on my foot?"*

Enough of that. That's sound from a different time.
The hum of marketing. The tiny tinkling of sales pitches.
Of campaigns and promotions.

Today's tinniness of likes and followers is not
the roar of production.
That's to come.
Can you hear it over the buzz and whine?
Move closer.
Need to.

> *"Move closer"*

> Phyllis Nelson. Echo
> chamber. Synth percussion.
> Tremulous vocal. '80s revival.
> Again. Not now but then.

Can I move closer to fashion?
Is it nearer now or just the reassurance of wishing it to be?

The comfort of proximity. The leaching of glamour.
A small puddle on the floor. But nearer.

Sound lures, sound beckons, sound draws.
Slides us up. Demands to be heard again.
Demands proximity. Deploys anticipation.
It's the best seller in the arsenal!

What next? What could be? What again?
What is it? What don't I know? What can I anticipate?

Generating the sound of fashion. No longer tinny
but getting deeper. Richer. More distinct.

Sometimes.

Phyllis and echoes of ads.
Fading.
All anticipation now.
Expectation, approaching, nearing, moving, closer.

Osun Bell Head

Cast bronze conical bell with human face in high relief with looped strap handle.

Vertical triple loop on forehead and ladderlike decoration present on cheeks and from both nostrils. Beneath, a naked human figure lies prone with hands tied behind their back, two birds pecking the head and legs.

Nigeria, tenth to sixteenth century,
copper alloy, lost wax process

Ringing anticipates appearance.
Ringing realizes ritual.
Ringing makes manifest.
Ringing beseeches.
Ringing implores.

Though made to ring and be rung, bells command worship
as soundless vessels, enshrined and vitrinized, yet
uncontainable, restless, weighted with the potential for
sonorous escape. Inert, they resonate silently. Mute bells
reverberate with approaching ringing, their noisy silence
triggering imagined pealing and cacophonies to come.

Worn to protect from witches. To chime. To time
ceremonial movement. The performance of becoming.
The procession of fashion.

Worn to make magic and medicine.

> *"When the leopard and the python wrestle,*
> *the bell will ring, and the witch will run away."*

Bells have shoulders and waists and lips and mouths
and crowns and yokes. Worn in the procession of fashion,
bells emphasize movement.

Officiating bells, sanctifying bells, hallowing bells,
summoning bells, bells shield, bells purify, bells mystify.

Bells sound fashion. Chiming the event.

Bells reflect evil back to the sender and out into the world.
Bells are apotropaic.

Bells must be kept bright and shiny to keep evil way.
To work magic. To summon. To entrance.

> *"Shiny shiny bad times behind me*
> *Shiny shiny sha-na-na-na"*

That decade again.

Bells conjure space. Ringing boundaries, borders and edges.
Fashion's margins and allowances.
Sonic space is slow and measured,
rhythmic and inevitable.
Fashion's cycles and revolutions.
Bells alarm. They warn of exceeding limits,
trespassing and transgressing.
Fashion's failures, disappointments and rejections.

Ring to recharge the sacral space.
Ring to guide. Ring to lure. Ring to lead astray.
Ring the bells to wake the gods, they are sleeping.
Ring the bells to drive away thunder and compete
with its clamor.
Ring the bells to cleanse the air and disperse the clouds.
Nothing must stop the procession.

Motorbiking.
Just one guardian bell for Harleys and Indian Motorcycles
(jingle jingle?).
Must be given never bought.
Must be hung below nearly touching the ground.
Ring the bell to capture gremlins.
Ring the bell to make them let go.
Ring the bell to horrify the demons and force
the witches to take flight.

Fifth

This look is most definitely born within the sound of Dutch Bow bells. "Who will buy" this chimeful, rhymeful, bell-laden costermonger's jacket? "Who will tie it up with a ribbon and put it in a box for me?" With borders and edges bell-free, it does double chiming duty as a blazer, fresh from the academy of Horsting and Snoeren. And who but our favorite Dutch hawkers would use that satin ribbon instead of a shirt as a cheeky tie? More cravat than full-on Artful Dodger bow, its fluttering ends leading the eye down to trousers, military-sharp. Bell defined. With brass instead of satin stripes, making these strides fit for parade ground and runway. Ringing, tinkling side seams make ready for modern-day Pearlies doin' the Paris walk.

> The fans go wild. Cheers from the terrace fashionistas.

Sixth

Back in the good old days hear the bells ring out the old and ring in the new with this Edwardian black frock coat and skirt. Ladies and gentlemen, lads and lassies, for your stylish satisfaction, I offer you this tintinnabular delight, a sonic confection! A pitch-black woolen two-piece, its edge-to-edge, hip-flared jacket free from sonics, providing a perfectly minimal counterpoint to the theme's main development, a skirt bounded and bedecked by bells. Here in the percussion section, shimmering sounds spill out from bells defining the hem and demi-bustle of this new percussive puffball. 1890s, 1980s, 2000s ... Ring out, you bells, ring out the years, and ring out a welcome as fashion's rotations take center stage for our listening pleasure.

Parisian bell artifice summoning the shades of European colonial acquisition. Benin, Ifẹ̀, Igbo-Ukwu. Now taxonomized into Lower Niger.

As if that linguistic regulation could diminish the bell head's deafeningly silent peal. Fashion. Here in the livery of Europa noisily scratches at and secretes shards of this ritual power. Claiming its anticipations and sanctifications for itself.

Lying in my bed at the age of four, trying, but not very hard, to get to sleep, I would hear Nana's ascent. Every evening my grandmother would make her way up the stairs to her bedroom next to mine. Increasingly unsure of her step, but insistently wearing her mid-heeled "mushroom courts," as she called the beige slip-ons she had a number of pairs of, and which were differentiated only by small details such as bows or broguing, she would tightly grip the banister as she made her ascent. Her progress was accompanied by a repeated metallic scrape and jingling as the two bangles she habitually wore on her right arm would jangle together when she slid her hand up the polished wood of the handrail. These two bangles, one of copper (worn to aid rheumatism, she said), was square in section and dented. I was never sure how it got so battered, the other cylindrical, shiny, silver and perfect, rattled and tinkled together, their noise getting louder as she reached the first floor and then proceeded along the landing past my room to hers. This noise was both comforting and somehow menacing, a jangling that I knew meant Nana, and yet was strangely disembodied, as if caused by a ghost. Those bangles were a remnant from her high fashion days in the 1920s, and which I later recognized in a few remaining photos, worn causally then, thin arms, boyish figure and closely cropped dark hair. By the 1960s they made the sound of her still, although by then, while her figure remained old-lady boyish, her hair was rinsed blue and sometimes violet. Part of her nighttime ritual included a few swigs from the dimple bottle of Haig whisky she kept in her wardrobe, and its pungent vapors would sometimes travel through the dark and reach my nose, another sensory pleasure following the bangle jangling. I loved her, she looked after me, taught me to play cards and made what she described as Melba toast, bread toasted on one side only, the other slathered with butter—a fatty delight. A memory collision of sounds, smells, fashion, food and fun that now, as I write this seem increasingly insistent.

Silver (jingling tinkling)
Golden (rhyming chiming)
Brazen (clamour clangour)
Iron (moaning groaning)

Oh Edgar, with your strangling collar and neckcloth.
Your casually knotted tie of prim shiny blackness.
Your tight little cutaway jacket and waistcoat.
Always buttoned at the top, then buttoned at the bottom.
The middle left undone to display linen-white midriff.
Such exposure, such vulnerability.

Edgar ever vulnerable to chimes.
Like the wedding peal when you marry your
13-year-old cousin.
Like the chimes that inspire you to write a
"Catholic Hymn" on hearing the Angelus.
Like the chimes that provide cold comfort
when tinkled within the casket.
Just in case. Just in casket. Just bells could save you.
Couldn't they Edgar?

But what a personal way of dressing.
Vest too tight because you've outgrown it?

                                                    Hardly.

Perhaps the constriction appeals. Or is it the grip
of fashion?
But no, no follower of fashion, no, rather a fashioner
of the self.
At least until dead at 40. Cause unknown.
Dressed in someone else's clothes.

What's that about dandies?
Something to do with pleasure gained from dressing
to delight the self?
Known only to the self, not for others, not for show.
No loud clanging but a barely audible knell.
Death of fashion, or death of fashion as we know it?
Long live fashion for the self.

Fine and dandy

Bells ring and here comes Mr. Baudelaire of course.
Admirer of Mr. Poe, much to everyone's dismay.
His *The Flawed Bell* an homage to Edgar perhaps with
all of his hearty tintinnabulation drowned out by the
soul whose ...

> *"faded voice sounds like the thick death-rattle of a*
> *wounded soldier who lies there forgotten near a pool of*
> *blood, beneath a great pile of the dead."*

Death of fashion.
Ring out the dead!
Long live fashion. But not for you Charles who dressed
only to impress ...
Yourself.
You of the sandpapered new suits.
Rasp rasp and tinkle tinkle.
The clinks of your oh-so-subtle toilette.
Can't be showy, can't be new, can't be *le dernier cri*.

But so much self-pleasuring in the echoes of abrasives.
On wool, serge, broadcloth, whatever.
As long as its nap is grazed, its luster lost,
its blackness faded.

And alongside the scuffing and rubbing came the copying
and the mimicking.
If you were happy with a suit you'd order a dozen copies.
No ringing the changes here. Just the inexorability
of repetition.
What an inspiration for that cortege of muffled,
of muted designers.
Herr Poell with your artificially worn-out dinner velvet.
Meneer Margiela with your replicas.
The dandy lives on despite the constant death knell.

"I heard the church bells hollowing out the sky,
Deep beyond deep, like never-ending stars"

Seventh   Everything's coming up roses for a perfect drape of
black crêpe. But this vision in black, despite its rows
of chaste covered buttoning, is no widow's weeds, no
tolling of death knells here. Instead, the sounds of
sophistication. This siren costume with subtle sonorous seductions outrings any lamentation. A single
oversized bloom, an extravagant rose of floral perfection rendered in palest amethyst gazar, defines the
waist and blooms below suggestive décolleté. Such a
merry widow! And, on closer inspection (who could
resist?), stiff and dusky mauve petals are backed,
bedewed, and bejeweled by a bed of petite pealers, a
myriad of brass bells announcing the cocktail hour.
Forget the Black Widow, I'll have a Pink Lady!

Eighth   Diagonal focus points to newly defined chiming hips.
Asymmetric hem on a sheer and satin striped shift is
encumbered by floor-skimming sash heavily laden
with bells. New sway dictated by new couture, its fresh
swagger announced by bold as brass bells. Perfect burden! Something kinda churchy going on here, as this
monastic black habit, relieved only by shimmering

self-stripe, prepares new fashion acolytes for a life of
perfect martyrdom. Real devotion is required to drag
its bell-heavy sash along cloister or salon, make way
for the new sonic religion!

The sound of the bells!
The roar of the crowd.
The show must go on!

Again and again. Enough bells. Abundant bells.
Repeated peals sound fashion's entrances,
fashion's exits, fashion's returns.

It's April 28, 1939, and Elsa is obsessed with music
and bells.
A death knell for Europe?
Warnings of exiles, of annexes, of annihilations
to come perhaps?
Music boxes hidden in hats bags and belt provide
the soundtrack and bemuse the audience.
Black silk chiffon tunic and gloves embroidered in gold
by Lesage

(who else, Elsa?)

with bells, bows, sleigh bells at pocket and wrist.

So many bells ringing the changes, so many bells
repeating the new.
Bell sleeves, bell-bottoms, bell skirts, bell cloches.
So many full-skirted cinch-waisted "bell-lines" echo
and sway through the annals.
And don't forget, bells have shoulders, waists, lips,
mouths, crowns, yokes.

It's 1951. Mid-century moderns chiming new lookers.

Give me Fath rather than Dior.

Who's tolling now?

We've heard all about V&R ringing in the new millennium
then four years later McQueen reprises their belled bodies
for Björk.

"*Who Is It*"

Muse, victim, clothes horse.
I want a dress that looks
like a bell
I want to wear it in
Hjörleifshöfði
I want children singing
in bell-studded suits
I want them ringing
handbells, I want a brace
of Siberian Huskies
I want what fashion wants.

September 2019. Wrighton knits boy's brass bell-strewn
cardi worn with mismatching sports socks.
All Fashion East protest and declamatory ringing.
Re-rung a couple of years later.
The charming and chiming cardi makes a comeback
for Nick Knight's face-filtering and glitching critique.
Such brazen simulation. Do digital bells sound so sweet?

Repeated peals chime down fashion's alleys.

It's July 3, 2023. Tinkle, tinkle goes Thom Browne's excess of haute couture with bells on. Bells on booties and bell heads (cloches mute and meaningless fade to gray next to bronze bell-head power). All beneath branded bell exhibitionism for one night only at the Palais Garnier.

Just listen to this …

> *"Time materializes as bells in cloche hats with reflective eyewear sway through the halls. Draped in three-dimensional trompe l'oeil wool tailoring fused with rounded tweed silhouettes made up of seersucker tulle, grosgrain ribbon, mélange pouf yarn, and sheer organza lace. With every step, a chime echoes throughout the theater."*

Hawking fashion

Fashion at the time of hawking.
Those pointy shoes. Call them what you will.
Poulaines, crakows, pikes.
Ludicrously long toes stuffed with moss
or horsehair to keep their shape.

Ungodly.

What do you do with such extravagant toes
when kneeling to pray?
No evidence they were really that big to need
chaining to shin or knee.
And certainly no evidence their points
ended with bells:

> *"Rings on her fingers and bells*
> *on her toes,*
> *And she shall have music*
> *wherever she goes."*

Why does the ringing of a bell sound of what is to come?
What is not here ...

Yet.

Surely the strident clanging is here and now, is not next,
but is present.
Why if bells summon and gather us does their ring bring
us elsewhere, to not here, to come?

How can such an insistent clamor be so immaterial,
so intangible, so ominous?
Mrs. Dalloway knows:

> *"First a warning, musical; then the hour, irrevocable.*
> *The leaden circles dissolved in the air."*

While whispers and echoes and tickings clumsily utter
other times and spaces.
Bells in their very hereness insist inexorably on
anticipation, on potential, on possibility, on the could be,
on the projected.

Nobody saw *The Schism*. My unseen 1980 St. Martins graduation collection was made of gray Holland linen, its sheen the result of a process called "beetling," where hammers repeatedly fall and rise, beating the linen into lustrous submission. I first encountered Holland, used in traditional tailoring as a lightweight interfacing, when making half a jacket in the evening tailoring class overseen by couturier Peter Lewis-Crown. Peter Crown was chief designer and eventual owner of the house of Lachasse. In his immaculate gray woolen coat and collar of what I naively named as Persian lamb, which he quickly corrected as "unborn lamb, dear," diminutive Mr. Crown, anachronistically contemporary, impossibly skilled and generous transformed my sorry demi-jacket under the steam iron. Turning my pile of black, clumsily padded and tacked stuff into something almost wearable that resembled half a jacket, I knew then instantly that I was no tailor. Anyway, for *The Schism* I stretched then varnished my Holland over a series of baby doll metal cages, crudely soldered and embellished with swags of latex and mineral specimens obtained from Eaton's shell shop, long gone, on Manette Street. The soundtrack I had envisioned, but which was never to be heard, was from the shower scene from *Psycho*, scored only for strings; Bernard Herrmann's orchestration was central to what he conceived as a black-and-white score for a black-and-white film. Throughout the strings are muted except for the shower scene, where suddenly, unmuted, they produce an unforgettably visceral screaming accompaniment to Hitchcock's vision of abluted butchery. A score so memorable that had I been allowed to show my collection, I believed (with 21-year-old arrogance) that my designs would produce an equally disturbing impact. Later, upstairs at the Chenil Gallery, long gone, on the Kings Road, *The Schism* was displayed as part of the *No Sacrifice* show, a sort of Salon des Refusés of banned St. Martins students and other assorted "fashion radicals" curated by my fellow student, flatmate, friend and soon-to-be celebrated fashion journalist Iain. This is him: "A show of strength by Tomorrow People—today," an early indication of his unique blend of optimism, love of pop culture (I'm sure *The Tomorrow People* would have been essential viewing for him) and belief in the power of fashion. Accompanied by its crowns of celluloid, miniature black opals and swags of pink latex pierced by aluminum plant labels, my collection was elevated on plinths. Art not fashion. Silent in its student optimisim, while downstairs the Blitz Kids' cortege progressed, oh-so-ironically, to Oldfield's *Tubular Bells*.

Ninth

The return of the crinoline. Bell-shaped pink sculptural drama swinging and ringing its joyous way. Unstoppable and unmistakably sounding this new season's resounding success. An insouciant marabou shrug blankets the shoulders of this bell ringer in an impossibly snowy drift of downy perfection. But that's not all! This foamy-topped raspberry milkshake is lashed with a sonorous sleigh-studded rope ending in swinging school bells. Break time's over. Now it's all about "Grasping the intangible," as our dapper duo demand, and to the sound of her seductive chiming all of our dinner-lady chatelaine fantasies come running.

> The crowd claps more consistently now. They know what to do. Or do they?

Tenth

An excess of bells carpets a floor-length coat of sable black. The merest breath of apple green internal edging subtly placed to echo the Grecian simplicity beneath, a column of verdant silken austerity caught by a slender lace of black ribbon. The weighty topcoat of brass and silver chimes keeps all present and correct. Sleigh bells swarm, are you listening? But this ritual procession is getting louder, heavier and harder. Bells ring the approaching culmination, sounding the difference, not long now. Long live the next. Happy and glorious. All hail the new sonic mode!

> Crowd now more claque than clientele.

Bells summon and sanctify.
Announce the mysterious.
Direct attention.
Waiting. Waiting. Waiting.
Building the buildup, the immanence of next.
Holy. Holy. Holy.

Willing acolytes committing their lives, their minds,
their bodies to fashion.
It is kept sacrosanct. No criticism is brooked, no charges
of irrelevance, no redundancy, no unsustainability, no
exclusivity mark the uninitiated, mark the less-than-
devoted, mark the ignorant, mark the excommunicated,
mark the loveless who form schisms while their clamor
will always remain orchestral color to the main refrain.

It is coming!

But anyway it's the Angelus that counts.
3 sets of 3 rings.
Approach.

It is coming!

The coming thing as bells prepare the ground.
Purify, usher, sound.
Where to look:

"Oh, noisy bells, be dumb;
I hear you, I will come."

Something impossible is happening.
Host and chalice.
Body and blood.
Ideas take on flesh, take on the mystery of creation.
I don't think so but ring enough bells and the crowd
will believe.
Ringing residue of effacement, of camouflage, of pretense,
of self-pleasuring.
Lost in the crowd.
No frow here.

Talking of sonic sustenance.
Talking of chimes and wine.
What about those 12 lucky Spanish grapes?
Las doce uvas.
12 grapes eaten at each stroke of the New Year's bells.
More than enough for fashion's diet of expectation.

But those bells again. The town crier's constant
companion ...

> *"who will buy [...]*
> *and put it in a box for me"*

Again.

Bells catalyze retailing, hawking, marketing, commerce,
consumption.

Fashion's bells.
Hear them foretell and compel of the rapture that impels.
Rapture made into sound.

Ravel's "La vallée des cloches"

(only as arranged by Grainger).

Used for *Tulip Time* but that's another room, another time,
another place.
Or for that matter Debussy's *La cathédrale engloutie.*

Ravel admired Poe ...
Loved his mechanics:

> *"the work proceeded, step by step,*
> *to its completion with the precision and rigid*
> *consequence of a mathematical problem"*

Baudelaire admired Poe ...
Loved his mechanics:

> *"I resolved to diversify, and so heighten, the effect,*
> *by adhering, in general, to the monotone of sound,*
> *while I continually varied that of thought:*
> *that is to say, I determined to produce continuously*
> *novel effects, by the variation of the application*
> *of the refrain—the refrain itself remaining,*
> *for the most part, unvaried."*

Not sure if Peter Lewis-Crown

R.I.P. ...

loved his mechanics but:

> *"My clients are discreet people who have no*
> *need to wear outlandish fashions to show that*
> *they are somewhere."*

Speaks of routine, speaks of order, speaks of cycles,
speaks of processes unseen.
Unseen too. Virginia, the House of Lachasse's miniature
wax mannequin would surely have brought 1950s glacial
glamour to Maurice's mechanical friends?

Change ringing opposes the single ominous strike as
bells are repeatedly rung in strict pattern and sequence.
Less music more a set of mathematical sequences.
Melody becomes calculus.
Delighting dandy Maurice, obsessed by carillons
and automata in his miniature valley of the bells.
Echoes echoing.
Rings ringing.

So too, fashion's endless repeats, its slight variations,
its monotonies, its backs, its forths, its versions,
its retrospections, its homages, its metavestmental habits.
Ceaselessly changing refrains that remain unchanged.
Its insistence, its calling, its marking of time,
its seasonality becoming its own refrain.
The sound of production, of mass production,
of the factory, of automata, of the best kind of model?
Dress dressing.
Fashion fashioning.

Maurice, Peter, Charles, Edgar.
Ring the sequence, repeat the perfection,
chime the pattern.
Edgar, Charles, Peter, Maurice.
The subtlest of variations, of almost inaudible,
of almost, but for …
Peter, Edgar, Maurice, Charles.
Strident, insistent, declamatory.
Charles, Maurice, Edgar, Peter.

Crowd gasps.

Eleventh Ostrich lining provides blessed comfort for a floor-
length, sleeveless, belled burden of a coat-cum-waist-
coat. Complemented by a diminutive train for extra

sonic gravity. Teeming with bells this tabard tolls its stately progress, forcing slow, unsteady movement. Lemon silk sash traps its weight and waywardness, as Ms. Kass, usual hip sway hampered, stumbles as she turns under its weight and the wait of anticipation. Bells, feathers, satin. Such a peal of plumage, its downy ringing momentarily muffled, like mournful mutes, but this is no funeral—*vive la mode!*

Twelfth Finale. Cowl-neck black evening dress belled at shoulder line, retreating to gold diminishing mini bell beads at hip line. Climactic restraint for this tinkling, twinkling beauty. Bells as bugle beads receding in hemline diminuendo. Glimmering. Upper jingling emphasis frames the perfect neckline. Sonic swags like classical drapery ring through the ages as past, present and future make sweet music. Ring out the eternal return, the refrain, the chorus of approval, as our last bells sound, chiming the denouement announcing the immanent return. Echoes fade, but never forever, listen carefully and you'll hear fashion's approach again.

Fashion is fed by anticipation
Fashion supposes
Fashion is speculative
Fashion converts
Fashion is ritual
Fashion transforms what was
into what will be
Fashion is summoned
Fashion repeats anew
Fashion is neophilic
Fashion interrogates redundancy
Fashion is difference
Fashion beckons

Frou Frou

Reached by a small passageway lined with tiers of silk frills that rustle as the visitor pushes their way through. Leading into a padded silk space, a luxury padded cell. A soundscape of rustling silk plays constant and low, like repeated whisperings or shhhhings. Intermittent visuals are projected onto silken walls. A small raised circular silk-covered podium for performance occupies the center of the room. All silk is of the palest pink or peach. The air is heavily perfumed with the scent of violets, tuberoses or perhaps lily of the valley, a floral fragrance evocative of the early perfumes of houses such as Houbigant and Guerlain.

Frou Frou.
Rustle of silk.
Riffle. Scratch. Whisper.

Noises too glottal, too back of the throat, too of things
moving through air and too rubbing against each other
to find words for.

                              The silky stuff of sex.

Cold. Quickly warming.
Slippery sensations offering little or no resistance.

Frou Frou, or Frou frou, or Frou-frou, or froufrou, or ...

Impossible. Inadequate word for what it evokes.
Or is it?
Say it with enough ffff before the rou and then
it might work.

            *"Say it loud and there's music playing,
            say it soft and it's almost like praying
            Maria"*

No. Blanche or even Fifi. Double f for fashion again.
But certainly not Maria.
Too saintly especially if you:

                  "never stop saying."

Frou Frou.
The sound of silk in layers, flounces, fluttering panels,
tiered underskirts.
Lustrous silk if you can afford it.

Cheaper stuff or even paper if you can't.
Paper-lined petticoats. Disposable but scratchy.
No matter it's the sound that counts.
Sound makes its entrance, sound heard before seen,
sound setting up the anticipation.
Fashion must always be about anticipation it seems.
Bringing and ringing us back to those preemptive
pronouncing bells booming in the other room.
It's the sound that excites, that stimulates, that arouses.
Induces sweat and panting breath.
Dogs for fashion.

                            The silky stuff of sex.

All this sonic salivating long before the glimpse
and even longer before the touch.
And for the wearer?
More pleasures of the self.
Pleasure gained from the knowledge of its power to
announce, to make an entrance, to manipulate the gaze.
The autoeroticism of sublimation and the animated
transference of frou frou.

Imagine the colors of frou frou if you will.
Rose. Pistachio. Apricot. Ivory. Gold.

White only if you must.
Saintly silky white is giving far too much vestal virgin.
Far too much virgin bride.
Maybe Prikker's *Bride* before her procession
becomes visible.
Before she walks down the aisle and makes her silky
presence known.
Rustling erotically in her incense-laden mist.
Swishing sensuously flanked by her phallic poppy grooms.

Frou frou mixing with bells in the heady vapors.
More Catholic than Viktor & Rolf's apparitions, but
nonetheless sonically sanctified and seductive.

No need to digress into symbolism.
We can take for granted that art is fashion.

                                                Can't we?

Fashion is art by now.

                                                Isn't it?

Let's get back to semantics, linguistics, semiotics,
onomatopoeia, phonics, timbre, noise, utterance,
primal scream, last gasp, cries, whispers, shhhhhs ...

Frou Frou.
Leave those capitals. They don't sound after all.
Unless a deeper breath is taken to add emphasis.
From now on frou frou and its insistent repetitious rose
rose, apricot apricot rustlings will suffice.

So despite the best intentions of Barthes and the rest
of the B team

        "Why does Fashion utter clothing so abundantly?"

The sound of silk against silk, the sound not the language,
the sound of fashion boils down just like the silk moths'
cocoons, to a nonsense, to a vanity, to a novelty, to a
gewgaw, to a frippery, to a furbelow, to a fallal, to a flounce,
to a falbala, to a fancy.

Fancy Frills

(more of them later when we
get to Spitalfields).

frou frou.
All the F words.
Fucking silk.

So, it was back in the '80s when my friend and fellow St. Martins student Sade asked me to design the set for her tour. The idea was that a series of big screens upstage should look like enormous, fabric-wrapped, rope-lashed panels. A bit like oversized parcels tied up with string, a bit like Christo. These wrapped panels, or perhaps parcels would be loosely draped so that where their silky volumes were caught up by the ropes they would make dramatic billowing shadows. In front of these would be risers and platforms of different heights giving the whole thing a slightly 1930s classically inspired film-set look, the look indebted to Vincent Korda's deco/fascist designs for the 1936 film version of *Things to Come*, which I had long been obsessed with. The silky, satiny fabric of these wrapped panels would, with the aid of fans, ripple and wave as if caught in a breeze, creating constant movement, and as I thought (perhaps overambitiously) a point of interest in the background. The effect of this fluttering drapery would be emphasized by dramatic, chiaroscuro lighting, and at a climactic moment in Sade's set, the drapes would magically cascade to the floor, the exposed panels beneath acting for the rest of the concert as projection screens. Well, that was the idea, anyway. Working closely with the lighting designer and set builder meant meetings at one or other of their houses, I can't remember which now, but I do remember the tortuously long tube rides to Hatton Cross, seeing and hearing the planes taking off and landing at Heathrow, and wondering what it must be like to live so near an airport. It was decided that the best company to make the draperies was the fabulously named King of Tabs, long gone now I presume as online searches insistently come up with King of Kebabs, no Tabs. Anyway, by this time after studying stage design, and working as a window dresser and prop maker, I thought I was pretty familiar with the properties of fabric. When it worked, my dramatic drapery idea was quite effective, however a reliance on mechanical, remotely controlled release mechanisms meant that the "drop" was not always as smooth as it should have been. Something about cloth and its vagaries has stayed with me from this early project, not so much concerning its physical properties, although the drama of a swag is undeniable, but more about how unpredictable, unanticipated and supremely seductive in their meandering reach textiles' journeys can be.

Due to centuries of being bred in captivity the silk moth
Bombyx mori is now flightless.
It doesn't eat, it is colorless, it now has no need
for camouflage, it is entirely domesticated.
It lives a cosseted, cushioned and must be noted
cocooned existence.

A life interior

> (drawing room perhaps,
> but that's for later when we get
> to the mise-en-scène).

Cordoned off from the dangers of the natural world.

No peaches, no puces, no periwinkle blues here.
Just leached parchment plush wings and furry bodies
the color of age.
Ironic really, given its adult lifespan of 5 to 10 days, most
of which are spent mating with human assistance now
a necessity.

> The silky stuff of sex.

The result?
Those precious eggs.
The laying of which is followed by death.
Hatched worms or larvae munch their Mulberry way.
Worms/Worth.
Clever, clever Zola

> (but that's for later too).

Let's keep it entomological.

Worms keep spinning while swinging in a figure 8.
Like the bees.
A mile of spitty filament trussing the promised
prized cocoon.
Or is it chrysalis?
Or is it pupa?
Such an abundance of words for pellets of candy-floss silk.
But before these fluffy Kinder Surprise containers can be
devoured and emergence allowed, they are boiled alive.

These downy carapaces. Now softened to ease
the release of 1,000 yards of silken filament.
Soft and softened gold joining up to 47 more such
strands to produce one silken thread.

                    Fucking silk.

What genus of fabric fancier (or better, what textile tyrant) on
first observing these fuzzy pellets imagined such material
wealth?
Could a mind be so attuned to species specialties
that unquantifiable moth-lives later frou frou and the
rustle of silk is the outcome?

And while lobsters scream in the cooking pot
Bombyx mori lets out subsonic frou frous.
Its gaseous rasps the silky sound of sex.

                              And death.
                              And treasure.
                              And fashion.

Does Ahimsa silk announce a different frou frou
where no cocoons are boiled, or steamed or roasted?
Is the frou frou of peace silk where moths flutter
free of a different register?
Is its mantra more melodic, more rhythmical perhaps?
Less abrasive, less discordant, or is that more or less
a cliché?
A ruffled chant less shot through with violence.
Whose rustle is less and less noticeable.
Watered down perhaps?

                                        But no.

Watered silk is showier.
Moiré's ripples the result of pressure and heat.
Lines of beauty maybe

                        (and more of them later).

But at what cost?
Any cost?

Without cost is the only acceptable way.
Gandhi and the Jains understood.
No moths accidentally inhaled.
Weren't we all unwitting Jains during the pandemic?
Countless miniscule lives.
The merest bug saved by the mask.
But not by the bell tolling amid the mass mortality.

Ahimsa literally lacking any desire to kill.
Shot silk shot through with refusal.
Mahatma's most effective weapon.

Mori moiré. Cruelty free?
No injury, no abuse, no oppression, no enslavement,
no insult, no torment, no torture nor killing can be
countenanced.
That's frou frou, that's fashion, and that's out the
window then.

                Fucking silk.

                The silky stuff of sex.

And what of raw, of shantung, of tussah?
Silk's mid-century modern cultivated imperfections.
Where slubs lead to slurs.
Is this frou frou rustling with the transatlantic twang
of modernity?
Phonemes modified. Drawn out.
Expressing similarity and difference.
Peace, violence, nationalism, *au courant*.
Is this frou frou in a lower register?
Slubs catching in the back of the throat.
Glottal stops and starts.
Brasher sounds with shades to match.
Lobster pink, heliotrope, emerald, garnet.
Harder silks look best in harder hues.
New techniques. Never subtle. Always make an entrance.
Silken whispers now strident.
Mauveine, fuchsine and Scheele's green.
Scream for attention.
La nouveauté.
Apple-green newphoria?

Speaking of modernity
Ms. Wilson and Ms. Taylor understand frou frou:

> *"a mass of exquisite flounced and frilled petticoat,*
> *which made the characteristic 'frou frou'*
> *sound of the period,"*

Or indeed ...

> *"the rustle of crisp silk petticoats [...]*
> *an indication of glacé silk linings rather than*
> *cheap cotton ones."*

With the sound so desirable and when glacé silk's out
of reach and quiet cotton just won't do,
does brown paper make an appearance?
Paper-lined petticoats. Disposable but scratchy.
No matter it's the sound that counts.
Lending bulk no doubt.
But most importantly the hankered-after rustle.
Or maybe crackle is closer.
A diminished relation to the papery crescendo resulting
from crushing and screwing.
Surely this is just the stuff of snobbery, surely warmth,
surely modesty topped any concerns about sonic *éclat*?

But Liz and Lou.
What of scroop?

> Surely not scrape
> and whoop?

An increase of rustling the result of the chemical
stiffening of silk and rayon rather than any woven
audibility.
Frou frou and scroop.
Textile talk perhaps, but lazy onomatopoeia provides
no explanation, and its signifieds are far too slippery.

Lost beneath the rustling of the demimonde, lost beneath
the layers of trifling excess, lost beneath the frisson
of flounced flesh, lost beneath silk, lost beneath skin,
lost beneath hair.
Rose and mauve the hues of silk and excited flesh,
and rushes of blood, and stiffenings, and swellings.

                         Fucking silk.

Is frou frou a vesteme?
Or is it beyond language or at least beyond classificatory
ambition?
Phoneme, morpheme, lexeme, vesteme.
Where has Sound gone?
Analysis leads inevitably to atomization.
The object under the lens is magnified to meaninglessness.
Not so the real repeated, the variable, the multilayered,
the stuffed, the crinolined, the volumes, whose dimensions
cannot be silent but insist on an unwritable ...

            cracklewhisperrasprustleswish

Instead sound distilled, sound sewn, sound embroidered,
sound ribboned, sound pleated, sound padded, sound
beaded, sound perfumed, sound sweated in, sound altered,
sound stained, sound worn, sound torn.
A merciless textile eroticism from which emerges a
semantics where sounds are basted to endless referents
that rustle apart only to be tacked together once more.

                    The silky stuff of sex.

Two still frames from *Münchhausen*, 1943

5 min. 48 sec. and 7 min. 14 sec.

Directed by Josef von Báky
Written by Erich Kästner

Distributed by Universum Film AG (UFA)

At 7 min. 14 sec. Münchhausen (Baron of Lies) flicks the switch "Licht auf" and shatters the silvery and silken landscape of Rococo Reich escapism.

Real silk or ersatz?

Beauty spot AND fan AND 1943/1785 stiff shiny old wig AND wartime lips AND that'll do / no one will care approximation of damask sprigs AND frou frou scrunched into Volksfilm AND relentless imperfections.

Glacé sheen as hard as iron as hard as mass destruction.

Sssssssssh.

Silk Frocks That Rustle

"FROU-FROU" DRESSES LIKELY TO SUPERSEDE THE SILENT FASHIONS OF TO-DAY

At a march of the mannequins, witnessed last month at a famous London dressmaker's, one of the mannequins created a sensation by filling the room with the pleasant sound of rustling silk.

It is many years since the frou-frou of silk was heard, and the women who were eagerly watching the procession noticed it immediately, and commented eagerly upon the fact.

Judging by the sensation caused by the rustling dress, it is not at all improbable that a new delight will be added to the gowns of the day in the estimation of the present generation, who did not participate in the frou-frou frocks that preceded the "silent" toilettes of the past few years.

Article from *The Globe*, April 17, 1912, p. 11

Back in the good old days, I got into video editing. Obsessively taping stuff from the TV I amassed a warehouse's worth of VHS tapes. Films, ads, documentaries anything (and everything) was captured, a process triggered by the sound of a program being announced, or a musical score that signified a film's titles were starting. This in turn set in motion the rapid muscle memory action of scrambling to find one of the blank tapes always at the ready on top of the VCR, inserting it and listening for the satisfying motorized sucking noise followed by a thud that meant the tape was loaded and "record" could be hit. As a kid I collected everything from Matchbox cars (my favorite being the Models of Yesteryear series of iconic vintage cars for which I constructed mini stages or showrooms) to beer mats, from gonks to the pictures (typically of women's legs) that came with the packets of seamed stockings my mother habitually wore, this last an analyst's dream (every pun intended) I'm sure. These pictures of seamed legs I assembled into a ring binder, the holes made in the images by a very old (probably belonging to my father) hole puncher, made of cast iron on a sturdy wooden base. The holes always punched perfectly, leaving circular confetti the color of stockinged legs, roses and satin bedroom accessories, the typical components that constructed these images. What this need to capture, to collect, to preserve stuff meant, I could have gone on at length about, because at the same time as I was amassing this "video library" I was teaching the psychology of collecting and had gotten very excited about all those programs that combined obsessive collectors and hoarders, and those turning their secondhand stuff into cash and decluttering both their living spaces and minds. At a similar time, around the late '90s / early 2000s, I was also using the tapes as source material for my PhD as well as for a collaborative video project titled *"Do you really want it that much?" ... "More!"* with my colleagues and friends, the artists Volker Eichelmann and Roland Rust. This looked at the popular image of artists, artistic creation, the gallery and art criticism in mainstream cinema. Situated somewhere between archival practice and institutional critique, the project went down well in Europe, especially Germany, featuring in group shows about archives, collaboration, film and representation. Anyway, my own work using bits of grabbed video imagery was transformed by learning how to use Casablanca, one of the first computer editing programs that consisted of a relatively simple storyboard method of editing. I delighted in assembling fragments of film, recorded from TV or that I filmed myself, accompanied by sound ripped from other sequences or from prerecorded CDs. The pleasure I had always got from playing records to images on TV with the volume turned down was suddenly intensified and I felt that finally my love of collage was fully realized by the Casablanca Series 1 system. The subject I chose for my early forays into filmmaking was textiles. Making textiles "speak," composing "scores" of cloth caught on preexisting film or newly filmed by myself provided me with endless possibilities for new narratives. Fragments of Spitalfields silk, stitched to the most banal cinematic visions of the eighteenth-century spoke of classifications, persecutions and the fragility of history. While Kashmir shawls trapped in museum vaults or draping painted shoulders danced with Bollywood, Hollywood and British film inflaming colonial desires and mercantile aggression.

Rustle. Shuttle back and forth.
Migrations and exiles all for fancy frills.
Alliances and schisms.
Textile transporters making silken waves.
The crash of the sea, the crush of the silk, the crepitations
caused as tabby, paduasoy, grogram, lustring, brocade,
tissue, velvet, satin and silks flee.

Woven silk

Taffeta brocaded in silver thread
Repeat, 72.5 × 53.5 cm

Spitalfields, 1742

Woven by Captain Peter Lekeux
from the design by Anna Maria Garthwaite

Rustle. Shuttle back and forth.
Migrations and exiles all for fancy frills.
Grantham York Spitalfields.
Le Havre Calais Spitalfields.
Textile transportation.
English French Francophiles and phobes.
Huguenots and Walloons:

"foreigners by 'inclination and kind affection'"

Anna Maria ...

> *"suddenly that name will never*
> *be the same"*

Garthwaite.

Pattern-drawer Garthwaite. Reverend Ephraim's daughter.
Mother Rejoyce. How did you learn your trade?
To mix and mingle. Styles, paints, colors, novelties.
1,000 designs sold, then woven with émigré expertise.
Lekeux captain of the richest flowered silks demands:

> *dark yellow plate*: strips of silver
> *light yellow plain*: silken core wound with gold
> *gray frosted*: textured threads that sparkle

frou frou.

> *"All the beautiful sounds*
> *of the world in a single word"*

A triumph of the will. Anglicizing that fussy France.

> *"the designs of the French have a poverty and*
> *embarrassment in them, to say nothing of the constant*
> *repetition of the same projects which tire and*
> *offend the discerning eye."*

Such hard silky condemnation.
Rigid grids enclosing Protestant and Catholic alike.
Brocaded persecution, lustrous discrimination.
Yet the line of beauty slithers across left and right,
weft and warp, Baroque and Rococo.

Hogarth. You and your lively S.
The line of beauty you make your Huguenot perform at
Noon. The posture of later frou frous, of Gibson Girls,
of any amount of Art Nouveau's whiplash whimsies,
of the rustlers on runways today.

Life-giving and vital S's that
Maurice and Verdine
reignite by ...

"Serpentine Fire"

Sidewinding back and forth from 1753 to 1977.

The S-word, silk, sibilance and ssss.
Lusssstring, tissssue, paduassssoy.
Say them soft and it's almost like steam.

S's into sounds, into figures on silken grounds,
into figures of speech.
Is there an in-between, between the threads, between
the sheets, between the shuttle throws? Where space and
sound thicken together and take on silken flesh.

The silky stuff of sex.

What's the matter with a repeat frou frou?
Patterns sonic, patterns drawn,
patterns woven need a repetition.
What about refrains, what about the chorus, what about
heddles and treadles, what about shuttles and pedals?

Making noise, making money, making the sound
of silken money.

Lustring Closely woven, very lightweight, extra glossy sheen from more textile violence, stretching, heating and soaking in beer. Dressed in your finest, night out on the town ending up in the gutter. Silk's sorry now. Originally only black, imports banned from France, English production strictly controlled, such is the politics of silk, but in 1718 when the Royal Lustring (Lutestring) Company is no more, despite the best efforts of, here he comes, again, founding member Lekeux, those settlers had silken fingers in every pie, black takes on more shade and is a firm favorite, especially in the Americas.

Tissue You'd think you know this one. But tissues have two warp and two weft systems, in modern parlance diaper and lampas, surely tissue with its central hiss is more sonically satisfying? Tissues the most complex, lace-like, and expensive. So tricksy effects are simplified by shady manipulation. Jacquard comes along and suddenly they are no more. The sigh of tissues now a barely audible white noise.

Paduasoy Eighteenth-century heavyweight, corded and embossed, technically could be a double tabby or a double tissue. *Peau de soie*, silk skin? Gallic sibilance bludgeoned by Anglophone approximation (I don't buy Padua). Stuff requiring a grand design as befits its ridgy bulk, more classificatory weaving as stuff becomes garment, silk becomes dress and, in the process too showy for the Vicar of Wakefield whose wife "retained a passion for her crimson paduasoy" despite his rejection of "rufflings, and pinkings, and patchings [...] flouncing and shredding."

Enough of all this textile dictionary stuff.
This play on words.
After all, there is an actual *Frou Frou* play, but you'll have
to hurry to book your ticket.
Fashion is fleeting after all.
Enough of this etymological finery.
Sounds of silk like sounds of places, of faces, of people,
of times, of shapes.
But not the sound of sound like good old frou frou.

But ...

> *"Hark! Hark! The dogs
> do bark"*

> Who'd have thought it?

Or rather I might have guessed that Duchamp very
nearly gets to the bottom of it.
On 46 scraps of paper jotted down from 1912 until his
passing in '68, *inframince* becomes his latest obsession.
Infra-thin *inframince*. The very lastness of things.
A final minimum before reality disappears.
Inframince cannot be defined and one only dares to give
examples he says.
For instance the whistling sound made by walking
in velvet trousers.
Of course this would be one of your examples
fastidious Marcel.
Swelling the ranks of Clan Dandy with Peter, Charles,
Edgar and Maurice.

> Already in the other room.

The sound or music made by the friction of velvet trousers in movement is linked to the concept of *inframince*.
So he says.
A silk velvet murmur as thigh rubs against thigh.

> *"Some in rags, some in jags,*
> *And some in velvet gowns."*

Silk and velvet.
So often seen, often sewn, often spoken together, often signifying excess and riches.
Frou frou and *inframince* what a double act.
One all rustling. One all whispering.

> The silky stuff of sex.

All that close listening

Motionless attentiveness to the merest whisper.
Catching the merest rustle.
The retreating sounds of stuff passing through space requires specialized sonic hearing.

Serres knows it. In *Les Cinq Sens*, he sounds out three types of hearing.
Hearing the noise of our own bodies, its internal tricklings, its gurglings, its beatings, its crackings.

Listen:

> *"Illness comes upon me when my organs*
> *can hear each other"*

Hearing the noise of outside, of clamor, of other people, of nature, of noise that approaches us, of noise that advises.

Listen:

> *"This noise resolves itself into information via the neatly complicated box of the inner and outer ear"*

And the third hearing is deaf to internal and external noise but listens to sounds with no name.
Perhaps no origin.

Nameless sound

Listen:

> *"surpassing the others by far,*
> *often to the point of cancelling them both out:*
> *silencing the body, silencing the world"*

Is this meaningless?
Is that the point?
To give up on meanings, on explanations.
Succumb to the senses.
To surrender to sound without rationalization.
Sonic immersion.

Trane and his ...

sheets of sound

Played it. Heard it.

Sheets of sound

The sound of sheets to be wrapped in, smothered in,
wound in, laid to rest in?
Sonic waterfalls, sonic blizzards,
sonic sand and thunderstorms.
And of course baptisms Mr. J. C.
Silken sonics flowing in never-ending ascending
frou frous.
Harmonically vertical. No simple linearity here.
All the chords, all the whispers, all the rasps,
all the rustles, all the progressions, all the sequences,
all the extensions, all the weaves.
The plaintive hoarseness at the point where
melody wears out.
The shriek where threads are pulled apart and rewound.
The warp set free from its weft leaving only
glistening strings.
But this is brass, remember.
Denser textures made now from weaves unraveled
in threes.
All those who hear are wrapped.

Are rapt:

> *"His continuous flow of ideas without stopping really hit me.*
> *It was almost superhuman. The amount of energy he was*
> *using could have powered a spaceship."*

The performer as Frou Frou stands on a slowly rotating silk-covered podium dressed in a gown composed of multiple layers of embellished silk frills. These are animated by Frou Frou's repeated smoothing, gathering, swishing and crushing movements, creating a soundscape of silken rustlings that rises and falls, sometimes barely audible, at others deafeningly noisy. Lines from the play *Frou Frou* are incorporated into the soundscape. This performance would take place daily, last 30 minutes and be heralded by the lighting in this space changing so that the podium is spotlit in preparation for the performance.

"What else is she but Frou Frou?
A noisy, bustling, busy little fairy—
ever rustling, rustling, like the leaves
stirred by a gentle wind.
Frou Frou, always; Frou Frou,
everywhere!
In the house a door opens and down
the stairs comes a rustling of skirts
like a whirlwind.
Frou Frou. Frou Frou!"

Extract from *Frou Frou*, 1869, by Henri Meilhac and Ludovic Halévy

Frou Frou, 1869. *La curée*, 1872.

Play and novel both equally obsessed with writing
the sound of fashion and the silken sounds of sex,
of avarice of duplicity.

Double frou frou

Zola fashions his novel with such silken skill as to
rival the great Worms.
His piss-take of Charles Frederick Worth.
Lincolnshire, London, Paris.
A thinly veiled gossamer disguise no more solid
than a moth's wings.
Zola writes fashion with silken words cut,
words sewn, words read, words heard.

Haute écriture?

Carnal confections rustling with Parisian putrescence.
Tailored in greed. The word and its gown made flesh.
Who needs the spectacle of fashion when you can hear
its sounds?

Apologies Émile but:

silk skirts glided with snakelike hisses over thick carpets (frou frou) there was a noise of chairs (frou frou) a flood of silk and lace surged through it (frou frou) a great rustling of silken dresses (frou frou) leaning back in her chair against which the satin of her bodice rustled gently (frou frou) part of a woman's silk or velvet dress flashed from an open landau (frou frou) pink silk woman standing before her (frou frou) shimmering in the hot light like watered silk (frou frou) sleep in silken sheets and take your pleasure (frou frou) along the satin of the couches (frou frou) a certain subtle link between cassocks and silk shirts (frou frou) such a strange voluptuous flower with silken flesh (frou frou) raising a silken counterpane and entering a huge bed still warm and moist (frou frou) when she opened the door again (frou frou) blue silk hangings stained with pomade and splashed with soapsuds (frou frou) while the silk of her bodice cracked (frou frou) she imagined tearing down the lace spitting on the silk (frou frou) gown consisting of a mauve silk polonaise and tunic (frou frou) dresses of silk shot with white flames and trimmed with satin frills (frou frou) silk satin velvet and lace had mingled their faint aromas with those of hair and amber-scented shoulders (frou frou) a nest of silk and lace (frou frou) the silk simulating rock showed broad threads of metal (frou frou) while closely woven silk seemed made for lovers of dolls and puppets (frou frou) silk had given her crime a coquettish quality (frou frou) the fragrance of flesh and luxury (frou frou) dresses undoubtably have a perfume of their own (frou frou) a changeable hue that altered from blue to green with a thousand tints of infinite tenderness

All this historical stuff.

Stuff

Such a good term for material, for fabrics, for matter,
for silk for that matter.
Silken voices speaking of the past, of the before,
of the not now.
Previous shouts and silences still sound the same.
Fashions fix. Fashion fixes the past but sound endures.
Silken rustlings rustle still.
frou frou then and now.

                              "Same as it ever was"

Four years following *La curée* along comes Renouvier
and his *Uchronie* or to give it in full, in translation:

            Uchronia (Utopia in History),
            an Apocryphal Sketch of the Development
            of European Civilization Not as It Was.

Not as it was or same as it ever was?
Silk sings both to us.
Counterfactual crooning non-time intonations.
frou frou then and now.
What ifs woven in.
Silken whispers of bodies gone, of bodies still,
of bodies to be formed.
The rustling of other rooms, of these rooms,
of rooms to come.

Sonic approaches from elsewhere but also here.
Immaterial.
Alternate but present.

Here it comes again

There it was in the distance yet a silk's touch away.
Hear it comes again. Always spot on Mrs. Dalloway nails it:

> *"like a faint scent, or a violin next door*
> *(so strange is the power of sounds*
> *at certain moments)"*

But all this to and fro. Back and forth.
Wafting in and wafting out wears the fabric thin.
Shredding and fraying and rending and ripping.
And we haven't even mentioned inherent vice.

        The silky stuff of sex.

Inherent vice, a built-in disintegration,
a shattering just around the corner or along the seams.
Seemed like a good idea at the time to make up for the
weight lost when sericin, the silkworm goo, is washed
from the fibers.
After all silk is sold by weight not by the yard
so give it a good dunking.

Bathed in metallic salts, silk gets lethargic, gets luxurious,
gets weighty, gets drapey.
A nineteenth-century fix for potential loss, a little
chemical enhancement making it all Worthwhile

      eh, Charles Frederick?

Reduced to tatters its silken threads are now ready for reworking.
Ripe for frou frou's return.

Production

3 interconnected spaces. Fabrication. Promotion. Consumption. The temperature is very warm, almost hot. Triggered on entering the spaces is a soundscape of textile and garment factory production noises, dialogue consisting of fashion promotion and critique ripped from mainstream cinema, and applause recorded at actual runway shows. This "soundscape" is formed of rhythmic sequences at different times overlaid, repeated, isolated and heard in unison almost as "chords."

1st space: Blacked-out room. Victor Burgin's *UK 76* print of a textile worker is pasted on one wall and spotlit.

Relentless rattling, clattering, backs and forths.
Seductively monotonous.
If a beat is missed something is wrong.

Needles, presses, shuttles, rollers, knives, hooks
and steamers.
Weaving, stitching, flattening, cutting, rolling and pleating.
The sound of fashion production is of a different register.
Pitches, tempos, rhythms, beats, pauses and repeats.
Manufacturing noise, manufacturing sound.

Its beginning, all crescendos and progressions,
all loud and overwhelming.
Its ending, all dwindling and waning,
all hushed and smothered.

Its noise now smothered, its clamor stifled, makes way
for the deafening silence of the image.
And so begins the magical salivation, the visual drooling,
the show me the next, and the next and the next.

After all, you eat with your
eyes don't you?

Visual consumption that's all that matters.
All noise of origin muted and forgotten.
See one more tempting morsel, one more visionary
confection.
Consumption's pandemonium screams for ever after.
Let's announce the "look at me!"
Let's predict, pronounce, push, clap and cheer.
All background noise to the look.
Mute production's pharynx filled now with c'mons
and shouts.
But what of the beginning's noise?

SpinningJenny1764WaterFrame1769SpinningMule17
79PowerLoom1785CottonGin1794RobertsLoom1822Se
lfActingMule1825HoweSewingMachine1844

What of today's?

Cutters

straightknifebandkniferoundknifelaserdieautomati
cnotcherstrimmersshearers

Sewers

singleneedlelockstitchdoubleneedlelockstitchpostb
edlockstitchcylinderbedlockstitchsingleneedlechain
stitchdoubleneedlechainstitchfinsihingchainstitcht
hreethreadoverlockerfourthreadoverlockerfiveth
readoverlockerflatbedcoverstitchcylinderbedcover
stitcinterlockersbuttonholersbartackersblindstitch
erszigzaggers

Pressers

BuckpressHoffmanpressvacuumpressingtableshir
tpresserstrouserpressersheattransferfusers

fabricspreadersthreadsuckerspulltesters

The sound of industrial production is the sound of the
new first heard nearly 300 years ago.

newmorenewmorenewernextnewernextnewmoren
ewmorenewernextnewernext

Producing sound. Sound production.
Profound suction. "De Profundis."

Mills kept hot to stop the thread from breaking,
kept hot to minimize cotton dust's explosive threat,
kept hot by windows nailed shut even in summer.
Breaths of lint and cotton dust and oil lamp smoke
fashion this season's lungs in brown.
The wheezes and rasps from byssinosis join
the industrial score.
Prolonged exposure to machine and mineral oil
manufactures a new line.
Let's call it "Mule Spinner."
Accent on weeping eyes, malignant mouths,
cancerous groins.

Production's score so loud that ears split and hearing flees.
Deafened workers refashioned as lip readers, signers,
guessers, soundless communicators.
Fines for talking and definitely no singing allowed.

Unproductive

Too normal?

After all Gracie trilled *Sing as We Go* only outside the
factory gates.

No chance.

Even with her register rising above the massed voices
of machines with their constant shouting, pounding,
thudding, clattering.

> *"Hee-hee, come on lads*
> *and lassies*
> *The factory's opened again*
> *Hee-hee, come on, Ee let's*
> *sing for it."*

So Gracie gets the factory reopened.
Silenced for summer its noise abatement now terminated.
Once more we hear it coming, hear it taking form,
hear the sound thicken, hear it take shape.
Repeats, refrains, rhythms, drumrolls, machine rollers
and snares.
Caught up in, getting lost in, childish limbs ensnared in,
mangled in.
"Scavengers" 6 years and up.
Crawl beneath the noisemakers clearing fluff.
Mending broken thread.

14-hour days offering so much opportunity for fatigue,
for error, for lateness.
14-hour days offering so much time for beatings,
for weighted necks, for ears nailed to tables.

The ruthless din drowns coughing, retching, screaming.
The relentless back and forth, forth and back stifles,
smothers, suppresses.

But then there's the hecklers, the flax combers,
the hemp teasers, the hair splitters.
The "over-dressed, loud, bold-eyed girls."
The shouters down and barrackers from good old Dundee.
Jutopolis. Woman's Town. She Town.
Hearing lost on the factory floor makes for loud talking,
makes for scowling and smirking, makes for drinking,
makes for making your voice heard.
Above the din, above the back and forth,
above the advance of technology.
Advancements like steam-heckling.
So much more cost-effective than hand-heckling.
Except no new automated hissing is heard.
Above the obstinate, the loud, the radical, the opinionated,
the Chartist, the organized, the jeering, the leering
hecklers.

Human din: 1
Mechanical din: 0

But hey, it's all worth it. For the newness.
As good old neophiliacs, black-shirted

(or at least black-suited)

Russolo and Piatti
perform with:

"ears more sensitive than our eyes"

On their *intonarumori* ...

3 howlers   3 roarers   4 cacklers   3 rubbers   4 bursters
2 gurglers   1 low hummer   1 low whistler

And Russolo shouts the new, shouts the odds.
Hammers home *The Art of Noises:*

> *"in places where continuous noises*
> *are produced (much-used streets, factories, etc.)*
> *there is always a low, continuous noise,*
> *independent to a certain degree of the*
> *various rhythmic noises that are present"*

And and ...

> *"This noise is a continuous low sound that*
> *forms a pedal to all the other noises"*

And and and ...

   (take a breath Luigi) ...

> *"some noises obtained through a rotary motion can offer*
> *an entire chromatic scale ascending or descending, if*
> *the speed of the motion is increased or decreased."*

And and and and ...

   (you'll have a mechanical breakdown
   if you're not careful) ...

*"orchestrating together in our imagination the din
of rolling shop shutters, the varied hubbub of train
stations, iron works, thread mills, printing presses,
electrical plants, and subways. [...] nevertheless,
our ear is not satisfied and calls for ever greater
acoustical emotions"*

Weeeee!

Or as Gracie would have it later, "hee-hee!"

                                                        More.

Do we listen to our clothes?
Can we hear their noisy origins?
Does the clatter, shuttle, thump, rattle,
hiss linger in threads, fibers and weaves?
Can there still be a resonance of the relentless sonic
driving, the crashing advance, the deafening patterns
of similarity and difference?

Hear Sylvester sing:

                    *"Over and over, time and
                    time again
                    Over and over and over,
                    time and time again"*

Hear Walter scribble:

          "Fashion is the eternal recurrence of the new"

Captivated by the journey of à la mode to outmoded.
Just like Luigi and his mob, turned on by noisy neophilia.
We crave the pattern of repeated newness.

New becomes old. Same and again.
Repetitions and redundancies.
Cycles shout the new but it's all bluster and brass,
smoke and steam, come and go.
Gone where?

                                          There.

Fort-da again and again and again.
The mechanical clamor for the next

                         (which is always the same).

On and on and on until the din becomes rings.

Not enough that work is scored by mechanization.
Non-work is also demarcated.
Stopped and started by recurrent ringing.
Punctuated by bells.

                                          Again.

But new bells this time.
Alarms, sirens, hooters, Klaxons signaling break times.

Unlike Cristóbal

          (never wore a watch,
          no publicity, please)

                    Balenciaga's site of production.
His famously white atelier was famously silent.
White noise perhaps?

The passing of silent white time regulated only by distant
chimes as he left like clockwork to attend Mass.

Summoned by bells.

                                        Again.

André

  (the strident
  overthrower)

      Courrèges remembers hearing him leave regularly
each day for the church on the Avenue Marceau.
Saint-Pierre de Chaillot.
Where long ago Baudelaire's and Proust's funerals were
held, but by the time Cristóbal made his bell-regulated
pilgrimages was brand new again.

                              All Catholic tradition and
                              machine-age decoration.

Then after the celebration of silent mysteries.
The return to the soundless sanctuary where slowly
cloth becomes clothing.
Still, save for the rustle of gazar, save for the whisper
of lace, save for the plainsong of tweed.
A speechless transubstantiation resoundingly
becoming fashion.
Each collection presented in sanctified silence.
Mute immaculate conceptions.

But all this silence is too much, too ascetic,
too pitiless, too much of the past.
Hail the new fashion sounds of clatter, crackle and rattle.
Of PVC, of aluminum, of rhodoid.
This must be new.

                    After all it sounds new
                    doesn't it?

Although echoes of those earlier sonic fascists can
be heard in Paco

            (dearest Mamá sewed
              for Cristóbal)

                    Rabanne's broadcast:

        "My clothes are like weapons. When they are fastened,
          they make a sound like the trigger of a revolver"

And with that Monsieur Courrèges and Emanuel

                                    (a devil in
                                double-jersey
                                disguise)

                                            Ungaro
seize the moment and stage their noisy coup.
Coast now clear as Cristóbal gives up the ghost.
His disciples fall away. His church disbands.
Alarm bells ring the changes.
And listen noisy new is back with a bang.

But just one moment. Noisy new is as old as the hills.
From factory floor to battlefield, au courant always
makes a racket.
Claps its hands, rattles its cage, blows its horn
and rings the bell.

Listen.

Hear.

Here comes cellophane. What a novelty.
Snap, crackle, pop.
A backdrop loved first by Steichen then for Beaton's
bright young things.
Fashionably artificial, glitzy and crunchy.
Then quickly before they fade, a spray of 1930s
freshest blooms wraps itself in cellophane.
Alix, Lelong, Rochas and of course Schiaparelli on a roll
with this miracle of modern chemistry.
Rhodophane, Sylphwrap, Kodapak, La Bourrasque.
Call it what you will but all regenerated cellulose.
Cellulose xanthate to be precise.

Good old noisy cellophane.
Nothing tops it as Cole pointed out:

> *"You're Garbo's salary*
> *You're cellophane"*

Crackling capes of "glass," of rustling jackets of cellophane
shag, of silent velvets interrupted by glistening strips of
noisy modernity.

Fashion loves this noisy novelty:

> *"The paradox of 1934: traditional line, fantastic*
> *materials—rubber, cactus, synthetic straw,*
> *tinsel, cellophane"*

The cavalcade of synthetic fashion scrunches on through
wars and booms.

Shiny, proud and noisy new.
But far away from chic transparency. Combining cellulose
with ease. British Celanese Ltd. perfects the artificial.

"Art" silk as good

                                        (nearly)

              as the real thing.
Just a little noisier.

Put Emanuel's, André's, and Paco's space-age antics under
plastic wraps.
We've already listened to their shake, rattle, roll.
While back on Earth everyone loves a plastic mac
and bin liner.
A momentary disposable din of do-it-yourself wrapping
soon smothered by designer sheen as Martin molds plastic
bags with added crunch and crackle from Sellotape.
And the Mad Hatter suffocates Galliano's rarest
couture flowers in yellow, rose and green cellophane.

Fashion's cellophane as Ms. Hawes had it back in the
good old plastic days when we first heard its seductive
crunch, recalling ...

> *"something slightly funny in watching them chase*
> *their own tails, done up neatly and gasping for breath*
> *in fashion's bright cellophane"*

All rustled up and ready to go. As noisy production
gives way to the racket of consumption.
The pitch of selling grows shriller as hawkers fill the air
with thickening word masses.
Proclaiming, swarming, deafening.
Howl the new.
Roar the next.
Cry the latest.

The shout of selling:

> *"is not a matter of tone or vibration but something not*
> *to be explained. It is a shout of pure evil, and there is no*
> *fixed place for it on the scale"*

Is it irresistible or can ears be stopped to its
ceaseless clamor?

An acoustic neuroma, also known as a vestibular schwannoma, or VS to its friends, is a benign tumor that develops on the vestibulocochlear nerve, which passes from the inner ear to the brain. The tumor originates when Schwann cells, which normally form the insulating myelin sheath on the nerve, malfunction. Was Theodor Schwann, son of a goldsmith, and devout Catholic, like Cristóbal, summoned by bells to his calling? To calculate the contraction force of muscle tissue; to find the digestive enzyme pepsin "a peculiar specific substance"; to explore yeast, fermentation, and spontaneous generation; to declare "all living things are composed of cells and cell products"; to discover cells that envelop nerve fibers. The Schwann cells. When functioning normally, Schwann cells protect the nerves that transmit balance and sound information to the brain. Sometimes "I wonder how I spend the lonely night" a mutation in the tumor suppressor gene NF2 results in abnormal production of the cell protein named Merlin, and Schwann cells multiply to form a tumor. Merlin, sorcerer or bird? I like to think it's the little falcon whose shrill, 4-second chattering call is the ornithological equivalent of the sales pitch. Anyway, this tumor is located on chromosome 22 in humans, 11 in mice, 17 in rats, and 1 in fruit flies. Unknown in a head of marketing. The tumor originates mostly on the vestibular division of the nerve rather than the cochlear division, but hearing as well as balance will be affected as the tumor enlarges. The most common early symptoms of these intracanalicular (IAC) VSs are gradual hearing loss, a feeling of fullness in the affected ear, imbalance, dizziness, tinnitus, or ringing in the ears. Tinnitus. Tintinnabulation. Hell's bells, Poe's bells are so persistent. Gradual single-sided hearing loss in the high frequencies is the first, most obvious symptom for the great majority of patients. Perfect for fashion shows. Blocks out the noise.

Fucking hiss, constant constant, overlaying every sound. Switch off? I can, but often can't. Forget it for a while, but not for good. Fucking noise!!! I first heard about it by a message left on the answerphone all those years ago. *This is a message for Jonathan Faiers we have detected a tumor in your ear.* Bed/phoneside manner—you gotta be fuckin' kidding me! So begins the stretching out of endless hours of partially heard TV viewing. Guessing the plot, missing the vital clues, missing the point. I prefer to have the subtitles on, but then it's all about the reading, not the listening or looking for that matter. Turn the volume up, OK for me—just—sometimes, but everyone else is wincing. So, telly has to be a solo pursuit now? But worse than that. Out and about. What a fucking nightmare. Conversation is now a battleground. Make it up, blag, wing it, but all so time consuming and not about hearing the other person, all about supposing, filling in the blanks like an endless fucking quiz game. Mostly get it right, mostly, or more accurately now, adopt a blank impassive countenance, no reactions (it's OK he's autistic, ha ha!). Sort of works but then I see the concern, annoyance or simply incomprehension as what has been uttered, declared, made audible meets with no reaction. A few brave ones say, "Did you hear me?" But that's as rare as hen's teeth, or rarer still hen's ears. Yes, they do have them. Lobes and all peeking from beneath the feathers, the color of a hen's earlobes are often the same as her eggs. But I digress, at the restaurant the Simon Says / musical chairs seating palaver starts: "Sit on my right, that's my good ear." "Sorry, I'm partially deaf in one ear." "Oh, so am I!" (No you're fucking not.) OK, as long as there's two, more than two I'm fucked, and table talk is like those redacted statements you see on legal / cop shows all blacked-out lines leaving nonsense or inconsequence. No longer the pleasure, in the moment, of talking with music playing, with other voices with any other fucking noise going on for that matter, as all upper/ higher/subtler sounds get cut out, censored, drowned. So, am I now supposed to only converse in and with lower registers? What the fuck, and then the overwhelming tiredness of the constant hum. Yes, it's there you thought it'd gone didn't you? Fat, fatty myelin sheath chance. Headphones, hearing aids all amplify but also then the fucking SSSSSSS is amplified too, so what's the point?! Outdoors is better, so should I live outside? Seaside waves provide blessed relief as their constant back and forth, crash and roar is the perfect extinguisher. I hear the space around me, I hear its limits or at least an imaginary set of limits bounded by SSSSSS. And then something shifts up or down a notch, but no, it's not that simple, something modulates. What a nice sonic concept for further restriction. Anyway, after the shift it's a different pitch, frequency, I don't know what it is except its SSSSSSS is somehow different. And then a new period of readjustment is necessary before I can begin to forget, ignore, fool myself that it's not there. Always compensations, always amateur lip reading I'm no good at. Facial expressions even worse. Endless ever-decreasing MRIs, *It's not changed, Mr. Faiers*, no you're right its size hasn't changed neither has the fucking SSSSSSS, that's a constant, polestar, true north of bloody frustration. Count myself lucky I suppose, it's not like it's proper cancer. Is this SSSSSSS why I'm writing this book? Is this the spur? Spur. Had one of them up my nose too, nosebleeds a regular treat, until general anesthetic fucked me right up. What is it with all these extra bits, bunions, ever-florescent moles, ocular pigmentation flecks, spurs, partial set of extra teeth for fuck's sake (becoming bruised budgie neck), schwannomas, 3 howlers 3 roarers 4 cacklers 3 rubbers 4 bursters 2 gurglers 1 low hummer 1 low whistler. Why the excrescences, add-ons, extra allowance for a garment that will only be worn by me? Appendices of functions long gone like the buttonhole in a jacket's lapel, buttons on its cuff, dysfunctional extras. I suppose I can say it's a reaction, can say it's about exploring/prioritizing the other senses, but deep down is it because the SSSSSSS sound is so fucking important and so troublesome, so constant and so unignorable? As I write this the SSSSSSS gets louder. What's the correlation? Creativity and dysfunction? Oh yes, ha ha! That old chestnut. Is it more physiological? As I type faster and faster the SSSSSSS tries to keep up, the relentless patterns, sequences and rhythms of sonics can't help but provide an accompaniment an undertone. Luigi's "continuous low sound that forms a pedal to all the other noises," the incessant sibilance of Disney stalwart Sterling Holloway's voicing of Rudyard's Kaa, the 100-year-old, 30-foot-long serpent, "trussssssst in me," the SSSSSSS of steam, rollers, pistons, pressers, compressors, hydraulics and pneumatics. Enough of this ranting. Against the SSSSSSS there is no therapy, so back to the sssssscribbling, back to SHOUTING the odds.

2nd space: White room stenciled with titles and dates of mainstream films featuring fashion shows, fashion promotion, and fashion statements and their costume designers, on walls, floor and ceiling.

Roberta, 1935
Costume design by Bernard Newman

The Women, 1939
Costume design by Adrian

Rebecca, 1940
Costume design by Irene

How to Marry a Millionaire, 1953
Costume design by Travilla

Lucy Gallant, 1955
Costume design by Edith Head

Designing Women, 1957
Costume design by Helen Rose

Fashion show. *Défilé*. Presentation. Parade. Runway.
All about the appearance. Look.
Yes there's music now.

But more or less of that later.

Not so long ago fashion was spoken.
Pronounced into existence.
Cuts described, fabrics labeled, effects declared,
locations imagined.
All silenced now except for the occasional revoicing
thanks to Monsieur Saillard and his walkie-talkies.

Models Never Talk but if they did ...

> *"Comme des Garçons. 1983. No makeup. Only dark eye-
> brows. Thick. Asymmetric. A long sleeve worn out in the
> end. Holes. A pocket on the strange volume. Long skirt.
> No high heels. Flat shoes. Black from top to bottom."*

Compère. Vendeuse. Host. Announcer. MC.
All about the words. Listen.
Best record now on film.
Scripted sartorial topography rules as looks
become places, parades announced, cloth defined,
critiques delivered.
Clothed in words from the golden age.
The show begins to speak.
A phonocentric pageant. Place and cut declared
one by one.

Name-calling, place stating, praise singing, soft selling,
value stressing, benefits peddling, dream vending, need
emphasizing, life changing, hawking, flogging, touting,
talking fashion.

> Fred and Ginger and Jane and Charlton take their
> seats. The vendeuse (or is it Mrs. Danvers selling
> someone else's clothes for a change?) welcomes us
> ...   "Bonjour, mesdames, mademoiselles. It gives me great
> pleasure to be your cicerone on our adventurous little voyage

into Fashionland." Lauren, Betty, Marilyn take a trip to see the *Rainbow over the Everglades* but run into a bit of *Trouble in the Afternoon* avoiding *Hard-Hearted Hannah*. Drowning their sorrows with *Double Frozen Daiquiris*, they laugh at the girl in Adrian's lilac-sprigged organza frightened by a cardboard bull entering stage left. Meanwhile, in Paris / St. Petersburg / New York, due to the smoke in her eyes and *Le Ciel Gris* Roberta/ Stephanie can't quite see *Le Petit Trianon* and is unaware of the "Peeled Eel" rushing toward her on *Le Train Bleu*. Next Norma, Rosalind, Joan move from the opera to the laboratory (avoiding the dreadful Crystal Allen). Edith Head beats Travilla and Bernard Newman to the mic and uses "velvet from France, organdie from Switzerland" and proudly announces "the return of the hostess pajama embroidered in Spanish jet." The governor. The real Mr. Allan Shivers applauds and the monkey (female of course) in the expressionist cage screams like a flute. How many liveried servants does it take to protect the woman who wears sable? Randolph wonders. And isn't it too warm for fur in the Café Russe? Meanwhile, Tom is trying to work out how many dollars it will take to get Pola, Schatze, Loco *South of the Border*. "Natural royal blue fox" in monochrome, "black cotton twill" in Technicolor, but none can match "all the iridescent colors of your Texan oil." However *Looky, looky, looky*, not every design makes the final cut. And the "spectator sports dress which converts into a one-piece play costume of jersey and checked matching wool," which, according to John Kent, who is more keen to promote his "Football line," is "the worst-looking thing I ever saw!" Fashionland is a dangerous place for the novice traveler, and even though "you will see the models go through the rhythmic movement of everyday life, and you will be able to study the flow of the new line as it responds

to the ever-changing flow of the female form divine," mistakes
are still made by the nameless girl who, on the advice
of the Comtesse Scharwenka, chooses green gloves
with metal finials and swagger coats with wooden
hands. No wonder Maxim asks, "Do you think that sort
of thing is right for you?" and remarks that "It doesn't
seem your type at all." But not to worry, Lucy Gallant
to the rescue, who reassures us: "As all of you know,
there is no one permanent fashion center." And so, as curtains
and cafés close and *La Sirène Noir* calls, we say *Good
Afternoon Sweetheart* and fade to black and white.

Name-calling, place stating, praise singing, soft selling,
value stressing, benefits peddling, dream vending,
need emphasizing, life changing, hawking, flogging,
touting, talking fashion.

So many announcements, pronouncements,
and proclamations.

3rd space: Blacked-out room with projection covering one wall
of the sound wave from a hand clap.

Sound wave from a handclap

Looped Schlieren image of a sound wave traveling outward at the speed of sound (767 miles per hour)
Courtesy Mike Hargather, *NPR*, April 9, 2014

Clap clap clap, clappity clap clap,
clappity, clappity, clappity, clap.

Claptrap. Trapped into clapping 'cos everyone else does.
The trap claps shut, it is done, it is approved, it is adulated,
it is worshipped.
Does the clap clap clap clappity clap clap keep the clothing
safe, keep it protected, keep the clothes cloaked with
safety sounds of admiration?

                              Or does it do more?

Does it sanctify, does it enshrine, does it protect,
does it deify?
Does the clappity clap clap clap construct a highway
of thunderclaps between our feelings and the product?
Clapped out almost.

                              But no.

The final appearance must be clapped.
Approval of the designer, not the maker.
Registered.
Sales foretold by declamatory clapping.

Clap and it is so.

The crack of a single clap, consumption's sonic aperitif,
consumption's nosily intermittent, consumption's rising,
consumption's falling digestif.

Oh, clap clap clap.

Claps echoing model footfalls, the crackle of stiffened
fabrics, the clatter of links, the jingle of buckles,
the rattle of jewelry all passed by.
Revive it from the dead, clap it into being,
clap it into revenue, clap it into endless promotion.
Clappity clap clap clap, with whoops, with whistles,
with hollers.
All wordless sounds, all sounds meaning something.

But what?

We like it? We want it? We will pay for it?
We like being like others, we like clapping our approval.
Listen as we clap, we trap, we squash, we explode sonic
bubbles of air between palms.
Oh the lack of rhythm, the lack of dexterity,
the variations of clapping.
From ineffectual pitter-patters to cracks that rend the air.
Puncturing and stabbing and smacks and cracks and
crescendos.

A clap is a hit after all. A blow and a success.
Like the clappers of bells.
Ringing and clapping can summon, can drive away,
can call up, can banish, can manifest, can atomize.
Flesh striking flesh.

> Hey presto, show's over,
> now let's eat!

Claps mark the end and precede the next stage.
Clappity clap clap clap gets the juices going.
Triggers the chic enzymes needed for digestion.
And excretion of course, but we're not talking about
that here.

> Are we?

That's back to the good old cycles eat, shit, eat, shit.
Season after season.
Collection after collection.
Happy clappers hasten the process, clapping the seconds
away, clapping us nearer to the final feast.

Clappity clap clap clap, clapped in sound.
Clothed in claps. Sonic enrobing.
Short sharp claps like itchy tweed, like scratchy silk,
like sweaty leather.

> But wait a moment.

Is all this clapping just applause?
It has all the plausible laudatory functions
and effects of applause.
Appreciation, recognition, approval, acknowledgment.
Even a form of tribute or payment.

It's the thing to do, the thing we have been taught to enact,
the thing that is contagious.
It only takes one clap to start a ripple that leads to a
cacophony and no one wants to be the first to stop.
But fashion's clapping is of a different register.

A deeper reverberation

Flesh smacking flesh is transitional.
Clap. Hey presto! Suddenly it's here.
Ready to go. Prêt-à-porter.
Devotees hitting hands, striking, attesting, certifying.
It is here, behold!
All that looking, all that spectacle, all that vision,
all leads to explosions of sound.
Wordless, spontaneous perhaps, ejaculations.
Applause is made up of claps.
But claps don't necessarily make applause.
We need a sound system to turn a crowd into an audience.

Talking of sound systems. We have music now, of course.
Specially composed scores, curated playlists. All that jazz.

                                        I wish.

Accompaniment or distraction?
Sonic interest to supplement tired visuals?
Noise to flood the void?

Can we imagine fashionable silence anymore?

In 2021 Demna tried in honor of Cristóbal.
In honor of the pandemic.
But the silence in 10 Avenue George V never stood a
chance against the din of:

Pronouncements:	*"We tried to step into those pictures from the past"*
Pontifications:	*"I didn't use my brain so much, I used my instinct"*
Propaganda:	*"For me, it was the beginning of a new era"*
Puff:	*"I feel at peace"*

The soundtrack starts up again.

If silence is out, what about restoring
the noise of production?
Film might help us hear, might bring us near.

The rebirth of textiles.
Synthesizing the noises of nascence.
No longer mechanical but chemical like our old
friend cellophane.
The Man in the White Suit was scored to a samba rhythm.
In 1950 sound editor Mary Habberfield blew through
glass tubes of glycerin.
Rattled brass and glass together and amplified
tubular bubbles.

Listen ...

> *Bubble, bubble, high drip, low*
> *drip, high drain, low drain*

Was the refrain.

The sound of cloth fermenting, the sound of stuff
congealing, the sound of fashion moving, the sound
of dancing even to Jack Parnell and His Rhythm's
"White Suit Samba."

Or you could leave music up to the imagination.
In 1946 fashion-starved "Max Boy"

> (Molyneux? Hartnell?)

> accompanied his
> unseen fashion shows.

His missing *Modes & Mannequins* with equally
insubstantial scores.
Flimsy sounds for flimsy frocks?

Listen ...

> *"Now follows something very different.*
> *The rhythm of a deep-sounding gong receiving*
> *a single gentle stroke, being followed by five sharp*
> *rat-a-tats on a small drum, and concluding with the*
> *unexpected solitary ting of a triangle being struck*
> *serve as a prelude to the showing of the next ensemble"*

Listen carefully

Before rebranded silences and unfinished symphonies
of pitch and pedal and push.
Before the ceaseless din of display and cries for the next.
Before transcribed scores and hit parades.
In 1836 noise was being manufactured,
and the sound of production endured

Come ...

> *"Enter with us into the large rooms,*
> *when the looms are at work."*

Listen ...

> *"The din and clatter of these five hundred looms,*
> *under full operation, struck us on first entering*
> *as something frightful and infernal, for it*
> *seemed such an atrocious violation of one*
> *of the faculties of the human soul,*
> *the sense of hearing."*

Bespeak

Dark oak-paneled room. Low lighting. A pair of large tailor's shears sits in a museum case on a plinth in the middle of the room. A looped soundscape of recitation of suit measurements and the sound of tailor's shears cutting cloth on a table plays. This increases in volume, reaching a deafening climax until commencing again. As the sounds get louder, the room dims and, on the walls and ceiling, multiple pairs of tailor's shears are projected with their blades sticking out and down toward the visitor.

Tailor's shears

ca. 1910–30
Pivot point marked WILKINSON & SON,
SHEFFIELD

Steel, Wilkinson & Son of Sheffield

Speak my body. Measure my frame. Clothe me with words.
Speak the garment, of the desires, of the lack, of the want.
Secrets spoken aloud.

Make me this, make me into this, make me, speak to me,
bespeak me, measure me with measured words.

	17"	22"	39"	17½"	3"	43½"	21"	7¼"	3"	31½"
Off left	31½"	3"	7¼"	21"	43½"	3"	17½"	39"	22"	17"

Length to natural waist from nape of neck.
Length to fashion waist if for a body-coat.
Full length of jacket or coat from nape of neck.
Half across back.
Sleeve length to elbow.
Length to cuff.
Chest measure taken over vest.
Waist measure taken over vest.
Stomach measure (in corpulent figures).
Seat measure (if this is not being taken for trousers).
Side-seam.
Inside leg.
Waist.
Seat.
Knee.
Bottom.

	17"	22"	39"	17½"	3"	43½"	21"	7¼"	3"	31½"
Off left	31½"	3"	7¼"	21"	43½"	3"	17½"	39"	22"	17"

All fleshy irregularities will be fabricated, disguised,
dissembled, concealed under cloth.
Dimensions voiced, widths noted, breadths repeated,
lengths checked, depths intoned.
Discrepancies, deformities, differences, asymmetries,
excesses and lacks.

All will be bespoken but oh so discretely.
Because my tailor, my body maker will *speak low*.

> *"Will you speak low to me?"*

Ogden Nash by way of *Much Ado About Nothing*.
What a lyric of lowered decibels.
But for me always Kurt and Lott[i]e.

Less lyrical. Reuben Sytner in his *The Art of Fitting
Gentlemen's Garments* notes:

> *"If one forepart is higher at the 'break' than the other,
> this will show itself at the 'break' marking-stitches. If this
> happens it may be [...] the customer is lower on one side
> than on the other, or has some deformity or figure peculi-
> arity which calls for both sides being fitted separately."*

But he does also advise the apprentice on discretionary
shorthand. Gently obfuscating acronyms.

> *sq.sh.: square shoulders*
> *sl.sh.: sloping shoulders*
> *sl.st.: slight stoop*

And subtlety to circumvent customer conceit, to reveal the true body, or at least the body to be worked on:

> *"Some customers unduly inflate and enlarge*
> *their chest when they are measured, and this is*
> *liable to cause the chest measure to be too large. To*
> *avoid this happening, it is advisable when the tape is in*
> *position to talk to the customer and ask him a question,*
> *such as: 'Is the tape too close?' He will answer and*
> *in doing so will exhale; this will cause the chest*
> *to assume its normal size."*

But before all this and after much measuring later
as part of ...

The Conversation

Cloth and lining and details must be spoken of.
Preferences, partialities, leanings

(this last measured accurately
and to be adjusted shortly)

are voiced, insisted on,
persuaded against, tempted away from, seduced by steel-
tongued sartors.

BESPEAK:

1. To speak about, to discuss (1489)
2. To speak for, to arrange for,
engage beforehand, to order
(goods) (1583)

Ancient longings saturate wool, fustian, broadcloth,
silk, velvet, linen.
While cashmere, tweed, flannel, worsted, mohair,
vicuña, gabardine, corduroy, moleskin, Merino,
all the Supers from 80 to 200 still stimulate magical
consumer salivation.
Cloth now conversed, let's talk the perfect body,
let's speak the character.
Say what you see, sew what you say, clothes maketh ...

                           And after, all the word
                           will be made flesh.

Clothflesh

So hard to write these sounds.
To describe this wordy wardrobe, to record tailoring,
to organize procedures of enfleshing.
Resort to other images, other noises, other comparisons,
other similarities, other contradictions.
To connections private and known, to likenesses
meaningful or meaningless, to good old fatty metaphor.

It's all there in *Sartor Resartus*, pompous yes, verbose
of course, fathomable only just.

Nevertheless ...

        "Language is called the Garment of Thought:
        however, it should rather be, Language is the
        Flesh-Garment, the body, of thought. I said that
     Imagination wove this Flesh-Garment; and does she not?
      Metaphors are her stuff: examine Language; what,
      if you except some few primitive elements (of natural

sound), what is it all but Metaphors, recognised as such, or no longer recognised; still fluid and florid, or now solid-grown and colourless? If those same primitive elements are the osseous fixtures in the Flesh-Garment, Language,—then are Metaphors its muscle tissues and living integuments."

My first suit was purchased in Rumford Shopping Hall. Can't remember the name of the shop. I say shop, but it was in fact really an internal market stall. On the right a wall of suits hung in two tiers, in a gap stood the owner, dim recollections, short, wore a hat? And I want to say a sheepie, dark brown suede with chocolate fleece. Always craved a sheepie, proper tan one with cream fleece, never got one though. Anyway, my first suit was purchased and to be worn to please my father, "one rule Son, clean collars, cuffs and shoes." The sound of the shoe-polishing ritual, a brush to put on, one to take off and the final buff with duster, a score that will never fade, made immortal due to the fragrant accompaniment of Cherry Blossom or Kiwi. The suit was purchased to look sharp (I doubt it!), to wear so I could be shown off at the Old Contemptibles dinner, and also "it will set you up," "come in handy in the future," and "you always need a good suit." My father coming from an older generation born in 1897 after all, the year of Queen Victoria's Diamond Jubilee, why his middle name was Victor, was full of such advice. Counsel from a simpler, more honorable era, some of which I still recall, some of which I have tried to follow. Not sure how good tan-colored Trevira, single-breasted, not too wide (for the time) lapels, flared trousers looked on my 9-year-old frame. And with hindsight now would definitely doubt its sartorial potential to "set me up," but I felt an attraction to it, liked how it looked worn with yellow-striped Ben Sherman, especially. I can still remember the sensation of standing bare-legged in socks and pants, squeezed into a corridor of suits ("Changing room? This is the changing room. I'll hold the mirror while you try it on."), padded shoulders rubbing against thighs, cuffs and buttons against face as the faceless "outfitter," no, tailor suggested room for growth and versatility. (How versatile can ginger Trevira be?) Not many memories of wearing it, a wedding maybe, or a steak dinner at the Berni Inn, then outgrown, useless.

Length to natural waist from nape of neck.
Length to fashion waist if for a body-coat.
Full length of jacket or coat from nape of neck.
Half across back.
Sleeve length to elbow.
Sleeve length to cuff.
Chest measure taken over vest.
Waist measure taken over vest.
Stomach measure (in corpulent figures).
Seat measure (if this is not being taken for trousers).
Side-seam.
Inside leg.
Waist.
Seat.
Knee.
Bottom.

Stitch my dreams. Sever the parts.
Disjoint and dismember and baste me anew.
This sartorial desire lives in the charnel house.
Parts dissected, cloth cut, ripped, pierced, sutured.
Ripped open again. No scars can remain.

All that vocal jointing, reciting of parts and their extents,
speaking of allowances and excesses.

>   (And speaking of allowances,
>   a tailor's yard always equals 37 inches.)

A parlance for impending butchery.
Preparation for the flattening, trimming, butterflying,
sectioning, boning, filleting, padding, spatchcocking,
packing, stuffing, drawing and quartering that will
surely come.
Flank, shank, rib, loin, rump, shoulder, leg, chest, waist,
seat, shin, elbow, coat, skirt, cuff, lapel, breasts (single
or double Sir?) (bodies or bodice?), scye, vent, dart.

All-consuming craving comes with all that speak.
Anticipation with all that placing, smoothing,
aligning, binding, bending, flexing, checking,
palpating, pinching, folding.

So much so we need Reuben's address:

> *"A man's anatomical formation will not permit him to*
> *wear trousers in the centre of his body, as a woman can.*
> *Because of this he has to wear them either to the right or*
> *the left of the centre of the body—usually it is to the right.*
> *If a man wears his trousers to the right of the centre of*
> *the body—as is usual—this means that he 'dresses' on*
> *the left, and provision should be made for his anatom-*
> *ical formation, or 'person' as it is called, when trousers*

are being cut. The right half of the topside is usually cut away; this is called 'dressed.' When the trousers are worn to the left of the centre of the body, this means that the wearer 'dresses right,' and provision for 'person' should be made on the right half. When such trousers are cut, the left half of the topside is cut away. In actual practice both topsides are cut wider and the side that is 'dressed' is cut away. Since the inside leg measure is usually measured on the right leg, one can notice whether the customer 'dresses' on the left or on the right. Sometimes the customer will draw attention to this; in any case a note should be made on the order form. Another matter which must not be overlooked is rupture. In this case the leg of trousers is cut lower and wider at fork."

That's clear, then. Thanks, Mr. Sytner.

But ... *"person"*? But ... *"rupture"*?

Is this a foretelling of the breaking up of the body to come, of its disassembling under lightweight wool?
As clothes maketh man.

Or simply groin strain?

If so then all of its attendant inside-leg vaudeville cackling is merely an attempt to coat the approaching sound of shears, severing, separating.

My first made-to-measure suit was from David London, 338–340 Hackney Road. Famous as the tailors that made many of Gilbert & George's trademark 3-button buttoned-up suits, this was and remains the best-fitting suit I have ever worn. David London took into account my "slightly rounded shoulders," a supremely tailored discretion, describing a stoop made all the more pronounced by a self-consciousness resulting from early adolescent growth spurts that paved the way for endless "Is it snowing up there?" comments or "For God's sake, stand up straight, Faiers" commands. My "hump" was cunningly disguised by skillful cutting—lower angle of shoulder line, jacket length longer at the back—it fooled me, and apparently others. Was I seduced by the art-world connection? Of course I was! The duo's understanding of clothes as art and life, as language, as deflection, as provocation seemed to me back then as Fashion Thinking par excellence, they were fashioned, fashioning and fashion. And anyway, they lived on Fournier Street, an address that chimed with the pride I took in my Huguenot ancestry and struck a chord with the textile histories I was pursuing at the time my suit was being cut. Talking of which, my suit, after The Conversation of course, was in medium-weight gray check wool with a blue line—went with everything, especially tab-collar shirts from Lewin's, when they still made beautiful shirts, and was styled to echo my naïve desire for a Sean Connery-era James Bond suit. Now whether this suit could be called bespoke I don't know or care, I had two fittings which seemed a surfeit of luxury and personal attention to someone used to off the peg, and it transformed me. This suit really was as comfortable as my own skin. I wore it everywhere. I wore it out. I wore it to be dressed up, to stand out, to fit in, to be ironic (or so I thought), to not have to think about what to wear, to give form to other layers worn over it, and of course for hatches, matches and dispatches. Subsequent suit spending at a much greater level never provided me with a better body.

Sartorial discourse is shaped by shears and the
act of cutting.
We think we are "looking sharp" and "cutting a dash."
The terminology of tailoring penetrates
with its "knife pleats."
An armhole is a "scye" or "arm's eye."
Such bodily displacement. Same root as "scythe."
Ruined tailoring that must be disposed of is a "kill."

Less directly violent and less mortal perhaps but
when uttered still cutting like a knife are all the

"bodgers"   (crude work of
                                   inexperienced tailors)

and "codgers"   (a tailor who does up
                                   old suits).

The "crushed beetles"   (badly worked buttonholes),

"cutting turf"   (more unskilled work),

"pigs"   (unclaimed garments)

and "pork"   (misfitting garment
                                   rejected by the client)

are "pigged"   (a lapel that curls).

While modifications on the road
to the perfect body/suit require

"tearing" or
"ripping down."

An expertly cut suit should not only subtly transform
the wearer's body but also be as comfortable to wear
as a second skin—and fit like one.
Our first suit of course being our birthday suit.
The one that still fits us best as we depart.

The linguistic play between these corporeal allusions.
The act of cutting followed by expert stitching delivers
us inevitably to all those cutters and stitchers both
fictional and real who emulate divinity while attempting
to create the perfect body.

Buffalo, Frankenstein, Gein cut to the bone
and tailored human flesh.
While Jack the Ripper Lee with his suturing and CCP
and his blood-soaked

"dead ends" and
"scar stitching"

struck a nerve and wallowed in the din of fashion's
applause.

The sawbones/stitcher schtick is always accompanied
by the speaking of parts, the clatter of instruments,
the recital of measurements.

The snip

Vasectomy or three-piece, Sir?

The rasp, the inexpressible sound of shears
opening and closing on the cutting table.

Surgeon Alexis Carrel (1873–1944) learned his techniques
studying lace makers. Click clack go the bobbins.
Perfected "triangulation" adapting the finest of lace
needles. Silent as they pierce for three stay sutures.
Traction points to minimize vascular wall damage
when closing up.

Did his lab really display beating hearts?
Telltale or otherwise

(hello again, Edgar)

as well as other functioning organs.

And so. What if in his black-walled cutting theater
he liked to cut a dash in black scrubs and mask?

Okay. Perhaps a bit too much Shelley and Karloff
led him to announce ...

"To progress again, man must remake himself.
And he cannot remake himself without suffering.
For he is both the marble and the sculptor. In order
to uncover his true visage, he must shatter his own
substance with heavy blows of his hammer."

Hammer blows, heart beats, snip, and rasp ...

"It's alive!"

Speaking, sewing, shearing.
The play between sound and silence.
This new body making. Declaring the form.
Tongues enfleshing organs of cloth cut accordingly.
Tacked, ripped open, healed again.
It's a noisy noiseless business.

But the sound of the shears, so sublime, so decisive,
so no going back now.

Swish?

                                        No.

Sssssh?

                                        Maybe.

Nasal and glottal retching, gagging, snorting?

                                        Sort of.

The sound of blades against cloth AND table together.
Duet or perhaps a chord of two?

A sheet of paper quickly screwed up.
Trudging through icy snowdrifts.
But metaphors and similes so lacking.

The shears breathe as they cut.
There is a pause before the next plangent slash.
A sonorous severing with a percussive counterpoint
of metal against wood.

Musicology also deficient.

Shear.

17" 22" 39" 17½" 3" 43½" 21" 7¼" 3" 31½"
Off left 31½" 3" 7¼" 21" 43½" 3" 17½" 39" 22" 17"

Length to natural waist from nape of neck.
Length to fashion waist if for a body-coat.
Full length of jacket or coat from nape of neck.
Half across back.
Sleeve length to elbow.
Sleeve length to cuff.
Chest measure taken over vest.
Waist measure taken over vest.
Stomach measure (in corpulent figures).
Seat measure (if this is not being taken for trousers).
Side-seam.
Inside leg.
Waist.
Seat.
Knee.
Bottom.

17" 22" 39" 17½" 3" 43½" 21" 7¼" 3" 31½"
Off left 31½" 3" 7¼" 21" 43½" 3" 17½" 39" 22" 17"

Tailor confessor, tailor creator, tailor transformer,
tailor maker.

Too much craft, too much inside information, too much
expense, too much cutting to the chase, to the quick.

So cover their sounds, drown out their drone,
their cutting, their ripping.
And speak against the tailors.

> *"It takes nine tailors to make a man"*

> (and one to ruin him,
> punned Walter Scott, living
> up to the cliché).

So a tailor is partial, fractional, not whole.
Dismembered in remembrance of the act of cutting.

Already deformed

Cross-legged sartorius muscles stretched to their limit.
Ankle bursitis.
Tailors' bunions at the little toe a specialized position
for the specialist in positioning.
Clothes may maketh but making undoes and deforms.
From the offcuts and scraps and remainders.

> Or might as well use
> the language,

"cabbage" and "crib" and "mungo."
A figure of fun is sustained.

Such venom, such calumny, such shit Shakespeare:

> *"Thou liest, thou thread, thou thimble,*
> *Thou yard, three-quarters, half-yard, quarter, nail!*
> *Thou flea, thou nit, thou winter-cricket thou!*
> *Braved in mine own house with a skein of thread?*
> *Away, thou rag, thou quantity, thou remnant;*
> *Or I shall so be-mete thee with thy yard."*

Ragpicker made of rags, body-maker made of parts.
Such claptrap, such snaring applause, such talking it up,
such talking it big.

But hold your noise about parts and limbs and scraps.
It's to do with bells

(here they are again)

and the dead.

Isn't it?

Nine tailors make a man.

Nine tailors or strikes of the bell begin the toll
announcing a man is dead.
Six for a woman, three for a child.
Three for a girl, four for a boy.
Now no longer secret as we hear it tolled.
So nine tolls make a dead man.
The strokes counted and told at the knells become
tellers bespeaking death.
Tolled into told.
Tellers into tailors at the tail end of the tolling.

So much corruption of words made flesh, of death
and flesh

(Nine, Six, Three).

Made sonorous by counting. Measuring, marking,
sound marking, sound making, body sounding.
Bell sounds mark and define space and orient and lead
astray and mark the passings and the becomings.

The body in Dorothy L. Sayers's *The Nine Tailors*,
or to give it its full hearing:

> *The Nine Tailors:*
> *Changes Rung on an Old Theme in*
> *Two Short Touches and Two Full Peals*

Okay, Miss Sayers, we catch the campanology.

Died suddenly. Foul play.
In Witham of all places.

Witham. Scene of Rose Hettie's relocation.
Rose deft tailor. Rose deaf to the Nine Tailors.
Not to their vibrations.

A surfeit of bodies, of assumed identities,
of patrician mania, of good old English xenophobia
sutured together with a fixation on change ringing.
Patterns of bells rung in precisely varied sequences
as arcane as a tailor's measurements, providing plot,
providing structure, providing social order.

Like a tailor, a bell ringer's numbers, runs and successions make the change, make the suit, make the change.

As mysterious as those sounded at the fitting of a double-breasted two-piece are the instructions for Kent Treble Bob Major. Normally the first method to be tackled after the simpler Plain Bob.

Words become sound; sound becomes stuff.

Place Notation: 34 34.
                    18 12 18 12 18 12 18,
                    18

Lengths: 32 rows per lead
          224 rows per course (7 leads)

Anyhow I repeat.

The body in *The Nine Tailors* ...

> *"His face has been terribly mutilated, and—
> what seems even more shocking—the poor fellow's
> hands have been cut right off at the wrists"*

Wears:

> "a suit of navy-blue serge of poor quality,
> much deteriorated by its burial in the earth,
> but apparently purchased fairly recently from a
> well-known firm of cheap outfitters; much-worn
> vest and pants, bearing (unexpectedly enough)
> the name of a French manufacturer; a khaki shirt
> (British army type); a pair of working-man's boots,
> nearly new; a cheap spotted tie."

No labels or tailor's marks to aid identification.
It is a body of parts partly French at that.

So if it takes nine tailors and it's neither their
nine parts nor the sound of nine bells tolling,
then is nine the number required to be truly
fashionably dressed?
To be truly partial, to be truly disloyal.
If we are to listen to Dekker's diatribe:

> "An English-mans suit is like a traitors bodie
> that hath beene hanged, drawne, and quartered,
> and set up in severall places: his codpeece in Denmarke,
> the collar of his doublet and the belly in France; the wing
> and narrow sleeve in Italy; the shorte waist hangs over
> a Dutch botchers stall in Utrich; his huge sloppes speakes
> Spanish; Polonia gives him his bootes; the blocke for his
> head alters faster than the felt maker can fit him and
> there upon we are called in scorne blockheades."

Cut that out!

Le style anglais will hush that noise, that silence,
that loud dressing.
The quartered body made whole.
But much shearing will be necessary.

                                        Again.

How to describe words for sound,
words for measurement, words for stitching?
But for cutting?
For steel sliding against steel.
Whistling? Scraping? Grating? Grinding? Scrating?
For steel opening and closing on wood …

                                   Words fail me.

Bespeak the body into parts. Cut the pattern and body
cloth. Former imperfections now sliced away.
And then once pierced, stabbed, sutured, basted, stitched.

                                   "It's alive!"

That shearing sound

So many reconstructed bodies resounding
under the blade.
Death. Dismemberment.
Rememberment by a thousand cuts.
Lingchi. Such Sinophobia.
Yet the process of making into parts so as
to be no longer whole after death still resonates.

That shearing sound

Only audible because of the correct alignment
of the blades.
Their perfect curve hammered into shape.
The handiwork of the putter or putter-togetherer.

                              The best name they could
                              come up with, evidently.

For the person who assembles shears. Putter-togetherer.
All those tutting t's an attempt to emulate the eventual
snipping sound but still not the sound.

That shearing sound

So many reconstructed bodies resounding
under the blade.
St. Agatha of Sicily, resolutely chaste, is mutilated
for her conviction.
She would not be remade or remodeled.
Despite sheared-off breasts

          (instruction for the Marquis)

                              miraculously healed.

Sanctified after death she becomes forever virtuous.
The unflawed body we hear made more perfect.
Beatified as the patron saint of Catholic bell ringers.
Bells as breasts?

                              Religious ecstasy re-tolled
                              as a sadistic joke.

That shearing sound.

Life cut short. Thread severed. Yarn undone.
The Three Fates measure and measure but it's inexorable
Atropos who cuts the lifeline with her shears.
Cuts out the end. Shapes the dispatch.
Trims the reputation.
Snip.
Surely a more cataclysmic inevitable noise is needed
for a life sheared off.

No such shearing sound.

Heard when cutting short the life of Swann
in *Dial M for Murder*.

But bells again.

Of the telephone variety this time.
Summon Margot, the modern-day Atropos,
to cut thread and splinter backbone.
Any sound of severing is drowned as the orchestra swells.
Blades brandished and plunged through the killer's flesh
and livery of gabardine trench.
Score rises as does Swann before falling back down,
driving the blades home.
Points embedded. Metal becomes flesh.

1994. At Goldsmiths as part of my art history and theory MA I had to devise a presentation. *Cast-Off* was performed by Dell and me in the same seminar room as I encountered museology, feminism and Freud. We set the scene with chairs, lamps and projected slides, the idea being to create a domestic tableau in which I gave an intentionally obscure lecture on linguistics and sexual politics, using the discourse of knitting, while Dell sat and knitted pink and blue (we knew it was obvious, but we also knew how to sell an idea) wool together. As slides including knitted outfits for Action Man, details of knitting patterns as examples of "new language," and Max Ernst collages with crocheted and knitted inclusions were flicked through, I rattled on and on. Lyotard and Kristeva, Barthes and Baudrillard, all the usual suspects were interrupted when I shouted "cast-off," the signal for Dell to voice my knitted memories. My Nana's front-only knitted tops (more bibs really) to be worn under her "costumes" and done up with ribbons looped over mismatched buttons—no matter "they won't be seen," and besides she would never take her jacket off in public. My failed attempts to combine wire with wool on the knitting machines at St. Martins—in retrospect was this an unwitting homage to Rei Kawakubo's dysfunctional machine knits? The ubiquitous sheep jumpers sold on Covent Garden market, where both Dell and I had run stalls, unaccountably popular. Surely not just due to the visual pun of wearing a jumper with the image of the animal the wool came from? There must have been something more to it than that? The mysteries of fashion (remember this was the first time around, not a retro '80s-revival kitsch thing), or perhaps the cult of celebrity: If Lady Di wears one then it's good enough for me. Anyway, these interruptions cut through the academic speak until I rose, overdramatically wearing my father's old suit, and cut Dell's yarns with my shears bringing the performance to an end. Applause from Carol, Jaimie, Barbara, Victor et al. The pleasure of bringing together different elements in this, our first public performance, has influenced everything I've done since, including this book, and anyway it helped me get a distinction ...

Jonathan Swift tailors his *Tale of a Tub* with such
abandoned shearing that the story/allegory/treatise/
polemic/parody or yet-to-be-named narrative garment
is repeatedly reduced to tatters, only to be basted
together again.

Digressions digress and endings begin and the
three coats lying at the heart of the tale are modified,
embellished, undecorated, worn out, worn in.
Cutting and dissecting and stripping shape this thing.

Hark ...

> *"Yesterday I ordered the carcase of a beau to be stripped
> in my presence; when we were all amazed to find so
> many unsuspected faults under one suit of clothes. Then
> I laid open his brain, his heart, and his spleen: but I
> plainly perceived at every operation, that the farther
> we proceeded we found the defects increase
> upon us in number and bulk."*

Savagery and ridicule and mutilation shape this thing.

Attend ...

> *"Another student struts up fiercely to your teeth,
> puffing with his lips, half squeezing out his eyes,
> and very graciously holds you out his hand to kiss.
> The keeper desires you not to be afraid of this
> professor [...] this solemn person is a tailor
> run mad with pride."*

So the clamor of fashion, the din of appearances,
the drone of measurement are conquered and succumb
to the hullaballoo of Bedlam.

And 30 years on from Swift's maddened tailor
he takes center stage in Hogarth's

(hello again, William)

asylum.

At the finale of *A Rake's Progress* amid the cacophony
of Bedlam, amid his companions, amid the wanking king,
amid the religious maniac, amid the voyeurs à la mode
squats the idiot tailor.

Wig of straw. Pattern pieces on his head.
Tape in hand now measuring nothing.

Any dimensions inaudible among the screams and sighs.
Suits unsaid. Coats undeclared.
Vacantly calibrating the ultimate guise known only to
him and certainly not for the naked rake in front of him,
now stripped of finery, now stripped of pretense,
now stripped of posturing.

In this noise the Bedlam tailor calls on his

Rock of eye

Guided by feel and intuition.
Following instinct.
Feeling the way.
More than all that measured precision.
Alongside the calibration and quantification.
A touch, a knowing, a feeling, a reaction, an imperative.
Is it from the eighteenth century, where we have been?
Or older, the fifteenth century, when it was *rack of eye*?
The track or path of the eye, followed and joined
by the other senses.

Je ne sais quoi?

> No. Too Frenchy for Bedlam,
> for Hogarth, for Savile Row.

Talking of madhouses, Val Lewton's 1946 production
Bedlam, starring Boris Karloff as sadistic and insane
Warden Simms, pays its debt to Hogarth and informs film
fans that it was ...

> *Suggested by the William*
> *Hogarth painting Bedlam*
> *plate 8, "A Rake's Progress"*

But in the shadowy RKO tableaux the tailor has
disappeared.
Out of sight out of his mind?
Maybe cut from the final edit?
More walling up than shearing in this madhouse.
Less measuring more disclosure.

For proper institutional cutting best to visit "Blind Alleys,"
the last *Tale from the Crypt* in Freddie Francis's 1972
portmanteau

> (your coat, Sir?)

> shocker.

Blind inmate George Carter trusting his rock of eye
implicitly implores coldhearted and luxury-loving
Major William Rogers, new director of the Elmridge Home
for the Blind, to turn up the heating as:

> *"With all due respect sir, we are not soldiers. Blind*
> *people are not like people with sight. We have lost one*

sense, but the loss of that sense only tends to sharpen the
others. Do you know what that means? We feel things
more acutely! If food tastes bad, it tastes worse to us.
If a room is dirty, we feel every speck. If an insect
scurries across the floor, we hear it. And if it's cold,
we feel the cold more."

Unmoved the Major in immaculately cut three-piece
suit and his German Shepherd, Shane, are punished.

Isolated.

Starved.

Major is force-marched along razor-bladed corridor.
Handiwork of the blind.
After nicks and cuts and the potential of worse
laceration to come

> (less cutthroat than *Un chien
> andalou* perhaps, but in the
> mundanity of Wilkinson Swords
> more inevitable).

The lights go out.
Major now sightless is pursued by starving Shane.
Runs the gauntlet of blades once more.
Suit and flesh reduced to ribbons.
Excessive cutting bespeaks the reformed body.

Bespeak:

> "For, looking away from individual cases, and how a
> Man is by the Tailor new-created into a Nobleman, and
> clothed not only with Wool but with Dignity and a Mystic

Dominion,—is not the fair fabric of society itself, with all its royal mantles and pontifical stoles, whereby, from nakedness and dismemberment, we are organised into Polities and Nations, and a whole co-operating Mankind, the creation, as has here been often irrefragably evinced, of the Tailor alone?"

Length to natural waist from nape of neck.
Length to fashion waist if for a body-coat.
Full length of jacket or coat from nape of neck.
Half across back.
Sleeve length to elbow.
Sleeve length to cuff.
Chest measure taken over vest.
Waist measure taken over vest.
Stomach measure (in corpulent figures).
Seat measure (if this is not being taken for trousers).
Side-seam.
Inside leg.
Waist.
Seat.
Knee.
Bottom.

CREDITS

BELLS

The bells! The bells!
They made me deaf, you know.
Popular misquotation from Victor Hugo's
The Hunchback of Notre Dame

"his coat, half red, half purple..."
Victor Hugo, *Notre-Dame de Paris* (Paris, 1831).
Translated by Frederic Shoberl as
The Hunchback of Notre Dame
(London, 1833)

Summoned by Bells
Title of John Betjeman's autobiography
(John Murray, 1960)

"Bonjour, mesdames..."
Dialogue from the film *The Women*,
directed by Georges Cukor
(Metro-Goldwyn-Mayer, 1939)

"Like the beat beat beat of the tom-tom"
Lyrics from the song "Night and Day"
by Cole Porter (Victor, 1932)

"Only you beneath the moon
and under the sun"
Porter, "Night and Day"

Standing Rock
Site of a series of protests in North Dakota
in 2016 and 2017 against the Dakota Access Pipeline

Idle No More
Protest movement that advocates for
Indigenous rights in Canada

"Here, 'twixt ..."
Betjeman, *Summoned by Bells*

"How it swells! ..."
Edgar Allan Poe, "The Bells"
(Philadelphia, 1849)

"Cooee! Cooee! Mr. Shifter ..."
Dialogue from P.G. Tips television
advertisement *Mr. Shifter*, 1971

"Move Closer"
Title of song by Phyllis Nelson
(Carrere, 1984)

"When the leopard ..."
Philip M. Peek and John Picton,
"The Resonance of Osun Across a Millennium
of Lower Niger History," *African Arts*
49, no.1 (Spring 2016)

"Shiny shiny ..."
Lyrics from the song "Shiny Shiny"
by Haysi Fantayzee (Jeremy Healy, Kate Garner,
and Paul Caplin) (Regard, 1983)

"Catholic Hymn"
Poem by Edgar Allan Poe
(Richmond, 1835)

"The Flawed Bell" ("La cloche fêlée")
Poem by Charles Baudelaire (Paris, 1857).
Translated by Francis Scarfe in
Baudelaire: The Complete Verse
(Anvil Press Poetry, 1986)

"faded voice sounds ..."
Baudelaire, "The Flawed Bell"

"I heard the church ..."
Betjeman, *Summoned by Bells*

"Who Is It"
Title of song by Björk
(One Little Indian, 2004)

Hjörleifshöfði
Mountain in Southern Iceland

"Time materializes ..."
Description from Thom
Browne website

"Rings on her fingers ..."
From "Ride a Cock Horse to Banbury Cross,"
a traditional English nursery rhyme

"First a warning, musical ..."
Virginia Woolf, *Mrs. Dalloway*
(Hogarth Press, 1925)

"Oh, noisy bells, be dumb ..."
A. E. Housman, "Bredon Hill," in
A Shropshire Lad (London, 1896)

"who will buy ..."
Lyrics from the song "Who Will Buy?"
by Lionel Bart (Deram, 1960)

"La vallée des cloches"
("The Valley of Bells")
Fifth movement from the piano suite
Miroirs (*Mirrors*) by Maurice Ravel, 1904–5

Tulip Time
Video by Jonathan Faiers, 1999

La cathédrale engloutie
(*The Sunken Cathedral*)
Piano work by Claude Debussy, 1910

"the work proceeded ..."
Edgar Allan Poe, "The Philosophy of
Composition" (Philadelphia, 1846)

"I resolved to diversify ..."
Poe, "The Philosophy of Composition"

"My clients are discreet ..."
Peter Lewis-Crown, *The House of Lachasse:
The Story of a Very English Gentleman*
(Delancey Press, 2009)

FROU FROU

"Say it loud ..."
Lyrics from the song "Maria" by
Leonard Bernstein and Stephen Sondheim, 1956

"never stop saying"
Bernstein and Sondheim, "Maria"

Bride
The Bride, painting by
Johan Thorn Prikker, 1892–93

"Why does Fashion ..."
Roland Barthes, *Système de la mode*
(Éditions du Seuil, 1967). Translated by Matthew Ward
and Richard Howard as *The Fashion System*
(Hill and Wang, 1983)

Fancy Frills
Installation and performance by
Jonathan Faiers and Dellores Laing,
HUB RiCHMiX Initiative, Bishopsgate
Good Yard, London, 1999

Things to Come
Film directed by William Cameron Menzies
(London Films Productions, 1936)

"a mass of exquisite ..."
Elizabeth Wilson, *Adorned in Dreams:
Fashion and Modernity* (Virago, 1985)

"the rustle of crisp petticoats ..."
Lou Taylor, *The Study of Dress History*
(Manchester University Press, 2002)

Münchhausen
Film directed by Josef von Báky
(UFA-Filmkunst, 1943)

Matchbox cars
Toy brand introduced by
Lesney Products in 1953

"Do you really want it that much?" ... "More!"
Video assemblage and installation by
Volker Eichelmann, Jonathan Faiers, and
Roland Rust, multiple versions, 1998–2005

"foreigners by 'inclination ..."
Peter Ackroyd, *London: The Biography*
(Chatto & Windus, 2000)

"suddenly that name ..."
Bernstein and Sondheim, "Maria"

"All the beautiful sounds ..."
Bernstein and Sondheim, "Maria"

"the designs of the French ..."
Malachy Postlethwayt, *The Universal Dictionary of
Trade and Commerce* (London, 1751)

The line of beauty
Key component of William Hogarth's
aesthetic theory as detailed in his
The Analysis of Beauty (London, 1753)

Noon
Second in the series of paintings
The Four Times of Day
by William Hogarth, 1736

"Serpentine Fire"
Title of song by Earth, Wind & Fire
(Columbia, 1977)

"retained a passion for ..."
and "rufflings, and pinkings ..."
Oliver Goldsmith, *The Vicar of Wakefield*
(Salisbury, 1766)

"Hark! Hark! ..."
Traditional English nursery rhyme

inframince
Marcel Duchamp's original notes on *inframince*
are kept in the Cabinet d'art graphique,
Centre Pompidou, Paris

"Some in rags, some in jags ..."
Traditional English nursery rhyme

"Illness comes upon me ..."
Michel Serres, "Boîtes" in *Les cinq sens*
(Grasset, 1985). Translated by Margaret Sankey
and Peter Cowley as "Boxes" in *The Five Senses*
(Bloomsbury, 2016)

"This noise resolves itself ..."
Serres, *The Five Senses*

"surpassing the others by far ..."
Serres, *The Five Senses*

sheets of sound
Term first coined by music critic Ira Gitler
in 1958 to describe John Coltrane's
improvisational style

"His continuous flow of ideas ..."
Liner notes by Ira Gitler for *Soultrane*
by John Coltrane with the Red Garland Trio
(Prestige, 1958)

Frou Frou
Play by Henri Meilhac and
Ludovic Halévy (Paris, 1869)

La curée (*The Kill*)
Novel by Émile Zola (Paris, 1872)

"Same as it ever was"
Lyrics from the song "Once in a Lifetime"
by Talking Heads (Sire, 1980)

Uchronie (*Uchronia*)
Novel by Charles Renouvier (Paris, 1876)

"like a faint scent ..."
Woolf, *Mrs. Dalloway*

PRODUCTION

"De Profundis"
Letter written by Oscar Wilde in 1897
during his incarceration at Reading Gaol,
addressed to Lord Alfred Douglas

"Mule Spinner"
Cancer of the scrotum caused by
prolonged exposure to mineral oils.
Prevalent among cotton mule-spinners

"Hee-hee, come on lads and lassies"
Lyrics from the title song from the
musical film *Sing As We Go*, starring
Gracie Fields, directed by Basil Dean
(Associated Talking Pictures, 1934)

"ears more sensitive than our eyes"
Luigi Russolo, *L'arte dei rumori*
(Edizioni Futuriste di "Poesia," 1913).
Translated by Barclay Brown as *The Art of Noises*
(Pendragon Press, 1986)

intonarumori
Experimental musical instruments
created by Luigi Russolo

"in places where continuous ..."
Russolo, *The Art of Noises*

"This noise is a continuous ..."
Russolo, *The Art of Noises*

"some noises obtained ..."
Russolo, *The Art of Noises*

"orchestrating together ..."
Russolo, *The Art of Noises*

"Over and over ..."
Lyrics from the song "Over and Over" by Sylvester,
written by Ashford & Simpson (Fantasy, 1977)

"Fashion is the eternal recurrence ..."
Walter Benjamin, "Central Park" (1939).
Translated by Edmund Jephcott and Howard Eiland
in *Walter Benjamin: Selected Writings*, edited by
Howard Eiland and Michael W. Jennings, vol. 4, *1938–40*
(Belknap Press of Harvard University Press, 2006)

"My clothes are like weapons ..."
Paco Rabanne interviewed in *Marie Claire*, 1967

"You're Garbo's salary ..."
Lyrics from the song "You're the Top"
by Cole Porter (Victor, 1934)

"The paradox of 1934 ..."
"Cellophane Shines in a Brave New World,"
Harper's Bazaar, March 1934

"something slightly funny ..."
Elizabeth Hawes, *Fashion Is Spinach*
(Grosset & Dunlap, 1940)

"is not a matter of tone or vibration ..."
Robert Graves, *The Shout*
(Elkin Mathews & Marrot, 1929)

"continuous low sound ..."
Russolo, *The Art of Noises*

"trussssssst in me ..."
Dialogue from the animated film
The Jungle Book, directed by Wolfgang Reitherman
(Walt Disney Productions, 1967)

"Comme des Garçons. 1983 ..."
Dialogue from the performance
Models Never Talk by Olivier Saillard, 2014

Fred and Ginger ...
All names, garment names (in italics),
and dialogue taken from the films *Roberta*,
directed by William A. Seiter (RKO Radio Pictures,
1935); *The Women*, directed by George Cukor
(Metro-Goldwyn-Mayer, 1939); *Rebecca*, directed
by Alfred Hitchcock (Selznick International
Pictures, 1940); *How to Marry a Millionaire*,
directed by Jean Negulesco (20th Century Fox, 1953);
and *Lucy Gallant*, directed by Robert Parrish
(Pine-Thomas Productions, 1955)

Pronouncements ...
Statements by Demna Gvasalia
from a series of interviews with Alexander Fury,
AnOther Magazine, Autumn/Winter 2021

The Man in the White Suit
Film directed by Alexander Mackendrick
(Ealing Studios, 1951)

Bubble, bubble ...
Written notation of the samba
rhythm devised for *The Man in the
White Suit* by Mary Habberfield
and Alexander Mackendrick

"White Suit Samba"
Song by Jack Parnell and His Rhythm
(Parlophone, 1951)

"Now follows something very different ..."
Max Boy, *Modes & Mannequins*
(John Green, 1946)

"Enter with us into the large rooms ..."
Anon., "An Account of a Visitor
to Lowell," *The Harbinger*
(West Roxbury, MA, 1836)

"The din and clatter ..."
Anon., "An Account of a
Visitor to Lowell"

BESPEAK

"Will you speak low ..."
Lyrics from the song "Speak Low," music by
Kurt Weill, lyrics by Ogden Nash, 1943

Much Ado About Nothing
Play by William Shakespeare, 1598–99

"If one forepart is higher ..."
Reuben Sytner, *The Art of Fitting
Gentlemen's Garments* (Tailor and Cutter, 1967)

"Some customers unduly ..."
Sytner, *The Art of Fitting Gentlemen's Garments*

"Language is called the Garment of Thought ..."
Thomas Carlyle, *Sartor Resartus
(The Tailor Re-tailored): The Life and Opinions
of Herr Teufelsdröckh* (London, 1833–34)

"A man's anatomical formation ..."
Sytner, *The Art of Fitting Gentlemen's Garments*

"To progress again ..."
Alexis Carrel, *L'homme, cet inconnu*
(Plon, 1935). Translated by David De Angelis
as *Man, the Unknown* (Streetlib, 2022)

"It's alive!"
Dialogue from the film *Frankenstein*,
directed by James Whale
(Universal Pictures, 1931)

"It takes nine tailors..."
Phrase traditionally associated with the
custom of ringing a church bell nine times to mark
the death of a male, but also conflated with the story
that Elizabeth I addressed a deputation
of eighteen tailors with the greeting
"Good day, gentlemen both"

"Thou liest, thou thread, thou thimble ..."
William Shakespeare,
The Taming of the Shrew, 1594

Kent Treble Bob Major and Plain Bob
Change ringing methods

"His face has been terribly mutilated ..."
Dorothy L. Sayers, *The Nine Tailors*
(Gollancz, 1934)

"a suit of navy-blue serge ..."
Sayers, *The Nine Tailors*

"An English-mans suit ..."
Thomas Dekker, *The Seven Deadly
Sinnes of London* (London, 1606)

Dial M for Murder
Film directed by Alfred Hitchcock
(Warner Brothers, 1954)

"Yesterday I ordered the carcase ..."
Jonathan Swift, *A Tale of a Tub*
(London, 1704)

"Another student struts up ..."
Swift, *A Tale of a Tub*

A Rake's Progress
Series of eight paintings by
William Hogarth, ca.1733-35

"Suggested by the William Hogarth painting ..."
Opening credit from the film *Bedlam*, directed
by Mark Robson (RKO Radio Pictures, 1946)

"With all due respect sir ..."
Dialogue from the film *Tales from
the Crypt*, directed by Freddie Francis
(Amicus Productions, 1972)

Un chien andalou
(*An Andalusian Dog*)
Film directed by Luis Buñuel, 1929

"For, looking away from individual cases ..."
Carlyle, *Sartor Resartus*

SPECIAL THANKS TO

Caroline Schneider and Sternberg Press;
Larry Lynch and the University of Southampton;
Iain R. Webb; Alex Coles; Nick and Matty of
Nickryanmusic; Michael Kelly and
David McKendrick Studio

Jonathan Faiers is Professor of Fashion Thinking at the University of Southampton, UK. His research examines the interface between popular culture, fashion, and textiles. Faiers publishes on a variety of subjects; his books include *Dressing Dangerously: Dysfunctional Fashion in Film* (2013) and *Fur: A Sensitive History* (2020) (both Yale University Press), and *Tartan* (Bloomsbury, 2008; revised edition, 2021), the conceptual framework for the exhibition "Tartan" at V&A Dundee (2023–24), for which he acted as consultant curator. Other projects include the cocuration of the exhibition "The Lore of Loverboy" at Somerset House, London (2024), celebrating the career of fashion designer Charles Jeffrey. His training as a fashion and theater designer and subsequent career in visual arts are fundamental to his interdisciplinary approach to teaching, writing, and curation.

Jonathan Faiers
The Sound of Fashion Thinking

Editor: Anita Iannacchione
Proofreading: Ciara Patten
Design: David McKendrick Studio and Michael Kelly
Cover photograph: Marius W. Hansen
Printing: Tallinn Book Printers, Estonia

Typefaces:

Le Jeune (Commercial Type)
Marist (Dinamo)
Jost (Indestructible Type*)
Forma DJR (David Jonathan Ross)
Times Ten (Linotype)
Clarendon Text Pro (Canada Type)
Snell Roundhand (Linotype)

ISBN 978-1-915609-70-0

Distributed by The MIT Press, Art Data,
Les presses du réel, and Idea Books

Published by Sternberg Press
71–75 Shelton Street
UK–London WC2H 9JQ
www.sternberg-press.com